2.1

HOUGHTON MIFFLIN

Reading
★ California ★

We're Standards Champs!

California Standards

Welcome to Reading!

Hello, Reader!

This year, you'll share many fun stories. You'll meet a cow, two pigs, three ducks, and a yak. You'll read about thunder and lightning and wonderful bats.

As you read and share, you'll learn many new words. You will also achieve the **California standards.**

What are standards?
Turn the page and find out.

Meet the Standards Along the Way

Standards are goals. For example, one goal is to listen carefully. Another goal is to write complete sentences.

These goals can help you read and write well. Your teacher will help you. The books you read will help you, too.

Standards are listed before stories, like this.

Look for **standards** in other places in your books.

Inside a Bakery

Have you ever stepped inside a **bakery** and smelled fresh bread baking? Have you wondered how bread is made? You'll find out more about what happens in a bakery in the next story. You'll even read two **recipes** for baking.

▼ Bakers prepare their **dough** and bake it early in the day, usually before sunrise, so that **customers** may have the freshest bread possible.

You Can Do It!

Each day, your reading and writing will get stronger. Before you know it, you'll achieve the goals for second grade!

▲ The **ingredients** may change, but the idea is the same: everyone loves a treat from the bakery.

◄ Most **cultures** around the world eat breads or baked goods. Almost all bread recipes use some sort of flour and water. The rest is up to the baker.

What else will you learn this year? **Let's find out!**

155

Visit Worlds of Wonder

Your reading books are full of interesting people and places. There are heroes to meet and children just like you.

You'll learn about towns and cities and subways. You'll read about firefighters and families.

There's lots of science to explore, too.

In fun activities, you can use what you know about numbers.

Math

Science

History

You're On Your Way!
Do your best work.
Listen to those who
can help you learn.
The reading skills you
learn now will travel
with you all your life.

HOUGHTON MIFFLIN
Reading
★ California ★

Adventures

Senior Authors
J. David Cooper
John J. Pikulski

Authors
Patricia A. Ackerman
Kathryn H. Au
David J. Chard
Gilbert G. Garcia
Claude N. Goldenberg
Marjorie Y. Lipson
Susan E. Page
Shane Templeton
Sheila W. Valencia
MaryEllen Vogt

Consultants
Linda H. Butler
Linnea C. Ehri
Carla B. Ford

HOUGHTON MIFFLIN
Reading
A Legacy of Literacy

 HOUGHTON MIFFLIN   BOSTON • MORRIS PLAINS, NJ

California • Colorado • Georgia • Illinois • New Jersey • Texas

Cover and title page photography by Michelle Joyce.

Cover illustration is from *Henry and Mudge and the Starry Night*, by Cynthia Rylant, illustrated by Suçie Stevenson. Text copyright © 1998 by Cynthia Rylant. Illustrations copyright © 1998 by Suçie Stevenson. Reprinted by permission of Simon & Schuster Books for Young Readers, an imprint of Simon & Schuster Children's Publishing Division. All rights reserved.

Acknowledgments begin on page 381.

Copyright © 2003 by Houghton Mifflin Company. All rights reserved.

Printed in the U.S.A.

ISBN: 0-618-15716-6

23456789-DW-07 06 05 04 03 02

Contents
Theme 1

Silly Stories

Phonics Library

- Len and Linda's Picnic
- An Ice Cream Crash
- Big Hog's House Hunt
- Robin's Farm
- Jane's Mistake
- The Big Surprise

Big Book

Cows Can't Fly
by David Milgrim
🎗 IRA-CBC Children's Choice

On My Way Practice Reader

Fluff and the Long Nap
by Misha Millarky

Theme Paperbacks

The Adventures of Sugar and Junior
by Angela Shelf Medearis
🎗 Award-winning author

Rats on the Roof
by James Marshall
🎗 ALA Notable Children's Book, Best Books for Children

Nature Walk

114

5

realistic fiction

Phonics Library

- Miss Pig's Garden
- Mike and Dave Sleep Outside
- A Trip to Central Park
- Zeke and Pete Rule!
- In the Woods
- A Snake Sheds Its Skin

Big Book

Time to Sleep
by Denise Fleming
🏅 Charlotte Zolotow Award Commended Book, CCBC "Choices"

On My Way Practice Reader

Animal Tracks Are Everywhere
by Misha Millarky

Theme Paperbacks

Amelia Bedelia Goes Camping
by Peggy Parish
🏅 IRA-CBC Children's Choices, Best Books for Children

Chibi
by Barbara Brenner and Julia Takaya
🏅 CCBC "Choices"

6

Focus on

Fables

Contents
Theme 3

Around Town:
Neighborhood and Community — 226

realistic fiction

Phonics Library

- Sunshine for the Circus
- Mother's Day Parade on Park Street
- Jay the Mailman
- Watch Out for Thick Mud!
- Mouse's Crowded House
- Hooray for Main Street
- The Clean Team
- Big Hound's Lunch

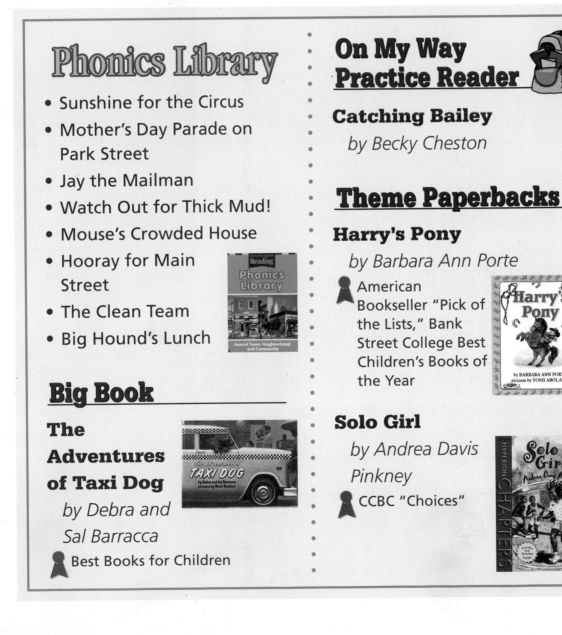

Big Book

The Adventures of Taxi Dog

by Debra and Sal Barracca

🎀 Best Books for Children

On My Way Practice Reader

Catching Bailey

by Becky Cheston

Theme Paperbacks

Harry's Pony

by Barbara Ann Porte

🎀 American Bookseller "Pick of the Lists," Bank Street College Best Children's Books of the Year

Solo Girl

by Andrea Davis Pinkney

🎀 CCBC "Choices"

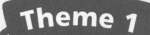

Silly Stories

Smile

It takes a lot of work to frown.

It's easier to smile —

Just take the corners of your mouth

And stretch them for a mile.

by Douglas Florian

Silly Stories

Contents

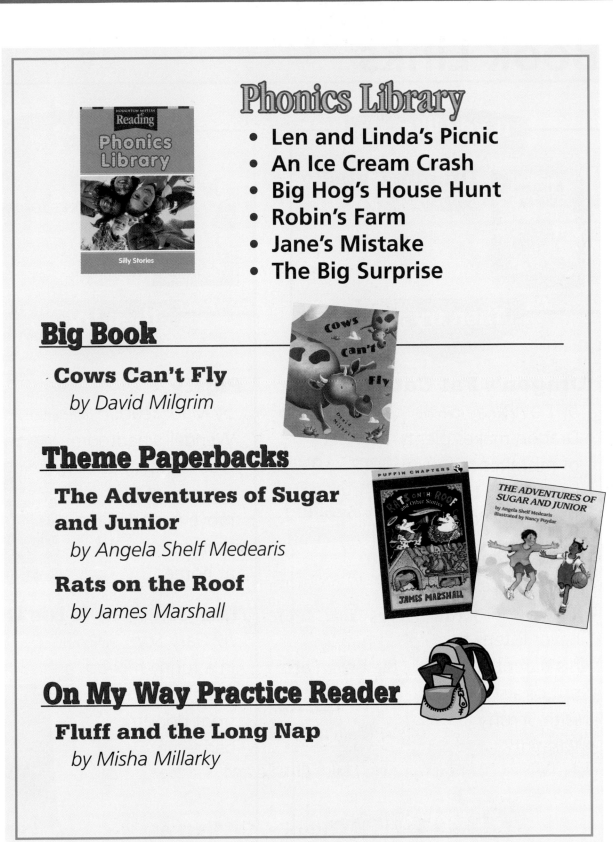

Phonics Library

- Len and Linda's Picnic
- An Ice Cream Crash
- Big Hog's House Hunt
- Robin's Farm
- Jane's Mistake
- The Big Surprise

Big Book

Cows Can't Fly
by David Milgrim

Theme Paperbacks

The Adventures of Sugar and Junior
by Angela Shelf Medearis

Rats on the Roof
by James Marshall

On My Way Practice Reader

Fluff and the Long Nap
by Misha Millarky

Book Links

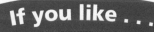

Dragon Gets By
by Dav Pilkey

Dragon's Fat Cat

by Dav Pilkey (Orchard)
Dragon makes plenty
of mistakes as he
learns how to care
for a stray cat.

Listen Buddy

by Helen Lester (Houghton)
Can a bunny who
never listens to
his parents get
out of a scrape
with Scruffy
Varmint?

Julius
by Angela Johnson

Pigsty

by Mark Teague (Scholastic)
Wendell's bedroom
is so messy that
a group of pigs
move in and make
themselves right
at home.

The Old Man & His Door

by Gary Soto (Putnam)
In a funny mix-up, an
old man brings his
front door to a
barbecue.

Mrs. Brown Went to Town
by Wong Herbert Yee

Then try . . .

Hamburger Heaven

by Wong Herbert Yee (Houghton)
Customers at Hamburger Heaven love Pinky Pig's new menu and its Stinkbug Burgers and Snailburgers Supreme.

Farmer Brown Goes Round and Round

by Teri Sloat (DK Ink)
When a twister hits Farmer Brown's place, cows oink and Farmer Brown cock-a-doodle-doos.

Technology

At Education Place

Post your reviews of these books or see what others had to say.

Education Place®
www.eduplace.com/kids

• • •

At school

Read at school and take a quiz.

Accelerated Reader®

• • •

At home

Read at home and log on to

Book Adventure™
www.bookadventure.org

DRAGON
Gets By

Dav Pilkey

California
Standards

Standards to Achieve

Reading

- **Restate facts and details (R2.5)**

A Balanced Diet

You are going to read a story about a character named Dragon. Dragon does not have a good **diet**. To have a **balanced** diet, he should carefully choose foods from among the different food groups below.

The next time you go food **shopping**, look for the food groups shown. Be sure not to choose too many foods from the last group.

Now, doesn't looking at all of this good food make you **hungry**?

dairy group

vegetable group

fruit group

bread and cereal group

meat, poultry and nuts group

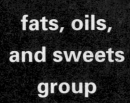

fats, oils, and sweets group

DRAGON Gets By

Dav Pilkey

Dragon's shopping trip turns out to be an adventure. As you read, stop now and then to **summarize**.

Reading   Restate facts and details (R2.5)

Shopping

Dragon looked in his cupboard, but there was
no food at all. "The cupboard is bare," said
Dragon. "Time to go shopping."

Dragon got into his car and drove. The food store was at the top of a hill. It was a very steep drive.

Dragon loved to go shopping. He was a very wise shopper.

He bought food only from the five basic food groups: He bought cheese curls from the dairy group. He bought doughnuts from the bread group.

He bought catsup from the fruits and vegetables group.
He bought pork rinds from the meat group.
And he bought fudge pops from the chocolate group.
Dragon had a balanced diet.

He had so much food that he could not fit it all into his car.

"I know what I will do," said Dragon. "I will eat some of the food now, and then the rest will fit in the car."

Dragon sat in the parking lot and started to eat. He crunched up the cheese curls. He downed the doughnuts. He packed away the pork rinds.

Dragon ate and ate and ate until all the food was gone.

"Burp!"

Now *Dragon* could not fit into his car.
"Oh, what am I going to do?" cried Dragon.
He thought and thought, and scratched his
big head.

"I know what I will do," said Dragon. "I will push my car home."

So Dragon pushed his car down the hill. The
car began to roll faster and faster . . .

and faster . . .

and faster.

Finally, Dragon's car came to a stop
right in front of his house.

All the excitement had made
Dragon very hungry.

He went into his kitchen and looked in the
cupboard. There was no food at all.

"The cupboard is bare," said Dragon.

"Time to go shopping."

Meet the Author and Illustrator

Dav Pilkey

Dav Pilkey is often asked why he spells his name "Dav" instead of "Dave." When Mr. Pilkey was seventeen, he was a waiter at a pizza place. He had to wear a name tag, but the label-maker was broken. Instead of printing "Dave," it printed "Dav" — and the name stuck.

Mr. Pilkey writes and illustrates his own books. He also reads a lot of children's books by other authors. His favorite authors are James Marshall, Arnold Lobel, Dr. Seuss, and Cynthia Rylant.

Other books by Dav Pilkey:

A Friend for Dragon, Dogzilla, The Paperboy

Internet

If you want to find out more about Dav Pilkey, visit Education Place.

www.eduplace.com/kids

Think About the Selection

1. Think of some helpful tips you could give Dragon next time he goes food shopping.

2. Why do you think Dragon didn't stop eating until all the food was gone?

3. Dragon ate all of the food he couldn't fit in his car. What would you do if you could not fit all of your food in the car?

4. Why do you think Dragon loved to go shopping? How do you feel about shopping?

5. **Connecting/Comparing** What do you think are the silliest parts of this story?

Informing

Write a Shopping List

Make two lists. On the first list, write the names of the foods Dragon bought at the food store. On the second list, write the names of foods you would buy at a food store.

Tips

- **Fold your paper in half as shown.**
- **Number your lists.**

Reading Restate facts and details (R2.5)
Writing Write legibly (W1.2)

Plan a Balanced Lunch

Make a menu for a balanced lunch. Pick food from the different food groups shown on pages 16–17. Name the food group each item comes from.

Make a TV Commercial

If Dragon were making a TV commercial for his favorite food, what would he say? Plan a commercial. Act it out for your class.

Tips

- Watch real TV commercials for ideas.
- Use describing words, such as *delicious* and *nutritious.*

Internet

Take an Online Poll

What are your favorite foods? Do you like to go shopping? Take the Education Place online poll and tell us. **www.eduplace.com/kids**

Skill: How to Follow Directions

❶ Read the title.

❷ Read all of the directions first.

❸ Be sure to gather all of the materials before you begin the activity.

❹ If there are steps to follow, reread each step carefully. Do the steps in order, following the numbers.

California Standards

Standards to Achieve

Science

- Objects in motion (S1.e)

- Predictions based on patterns (S4.a)

Roly-Poly

by Janice VanCleave

JANICE VANCLEAVE'S
Play and Find Out
about
Science
Easy Experiments
for Young Children

I wonder . . . Why do things roll downhill?

Let's find out!

Round up these things:

- ✔ baby powder
- ✔ cookie sheet
- ✔ coffee can
- ✔ masking tape
- ✔ ¼ cup tap water
- ✔ red food coloring
- ✔ coffee cup
- ✔ spoon
- ✔ eyedropper

1. Spread a thin layer of baby powder over the surface of the cookie sheet.

 2. Place the cookie sheet on the floor.

 3. Raise one end of the cookie sheet and rest it on the rim of the coffee can.

 4. Secure the cookie sheet to the can with tape.

5. Put the water and 10 drops of food coloring in the cup. Stir.

 6. Fill the eyedropper with colored water.

 7. Practice squeezing drops of colored water back into the cup until you can easily squeeze one drop at a time.

 8. Sit next to the raised end of the powdered cookie sheet. Hold the eyedropper just above the raised end of the cookie sheet.

9. Squeeze out 1 drop of colored water and watch it roll down the powdered cookie sheet. It will become covered with powder and form a round rolling object that we'll call a roly-poly.

Bow wow!

So now we know ...

Gravity is the force that makes things fall to the ground. It also makes round things such as balls and bike wheels roll downhill. That is why your roly-poly rolled down the cookie sheet.

A Story

A story tells about something that is made-up. It has a main character, a beginning, a middle, and an end. Use this student's writing as a model when you write a story of your own.

Ice Cream

Be sure your **title** makes the reader want to read your story.

The Hungry Panther

On Monday after school, I sat down at my desk. I wanted to finish my drawing of a panther. I got out my purple, black, and blue markers and started to color. Just then, I noticed my panther blink. Or did it? I got scared and ran to tell my mom. She gave me that look. I felt as if she didn't believe me.

The **beginning** of a story tells when and where it takes place.

That night, I heard a noise downstairs. I got my dad's metal baseball bat from the closet and went downstairs. I saw a blue, black, and purple shape. Then I knew. It was my panther causing the noise. He was in the kitchen making a turkey sandwich!

Help the reader picture the main **character**. Give details.

Writing
Write brief narratives (W2.1)
Write a sequence of events (W2.1.a)

My panther looked at me and asked, "Do you know where the mustard is?" I was so shocked that I went to my room and got dressed.

My panther and I walked to the ice-cream store. He ate three scoops of vanilla. I ate two scoops of bubble-gum ice cream. On the way home I fell asleep on the panther's back.

The next morning I woke up. I was already dressed for school. My mouth tasted like bubble-gum ice cream. Could this happen to you? Did this really happen to me?

> **Dialogue** makes characters come alive.

> The **middle** of a story tells the main events.

> The **ending** brings the story to a close. It can surprise you.

Meet the Author

Ashley C.

Grade: two

State: New York

Hobbies: swimming, riding her bike

What she'd like to be when she grows up: a veterinarian

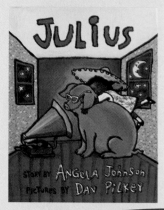

Julius

STORY BY ANGELA JOHNSON
PICTURES BY DAV PILKEY

California Standards

Standards to Achieve

Reading

• **Use short *o*, *u*, *e* spellings (R1.1)**

How Real Pigs Act

What does it mean to act like a pig? Have you ever seen anyone do an imitation of a pig? Do you think that's how pigs really act? In the next story, you'll meet a pig that acts more like a person!

These little piggies **slurped** their food.

Real pigs sometimes **spread** their food out and make **messes** while they eat.

Real pigs will eat **crumbs** and leftover food, but only if that's what they're fed.

Grunt!

Real pigs make a **noise** called a grunt.

45

Meet the Author
Angela Johnson

Born: June 18 in Tuskegee, Alabama

Where she lives now: Kent, Ohio

Hobbies: Watching old movies, gardening, traveling

When she began writing: "I started writing when I was nine. My parents bought me a diary. I wrote in it every day, mostly about my friends."

Other books: *The Leaving Morning, The Rolling Store, One of Three*

Meet the Illustrator
Dav Pilkey

Born: March 4 in Cleveland, Ohio

Where he lives now: Eugene, Oregon

Pets: He owns three dogs and one cat.

He once had three mice named Rabies, Flash, and Dwayne, but he had to give them away when he moved to Oregon.

Internet

To find out more about Angela Johnson and Dav Pilkey, visit Education Place.

www.eduplace.com/kids

JULIUS

STORY BY ANGELA JOHNSON
PICTURES BY DAV PILKEY

Strategy Focus

While you read about Maya and Julius, **monitor** how well you understand the story. If you're not sure about something, reread or read ahead to **clarify**.

Maya's granddaddy lived in Alabama, but
wintered in Alaska.

He told Maya that was the reason he liked ice
cubes in his coffee.

On one of Granddaddy's visits from
Alaska, he brought a crate.
A surprise for Maya!
"Something that will teach you fun and
sharing." Granddaddy smiled. "Something
for my special you."

49

Maya hoped it was a horse or an older brother.
She'd always wanted one or the other.

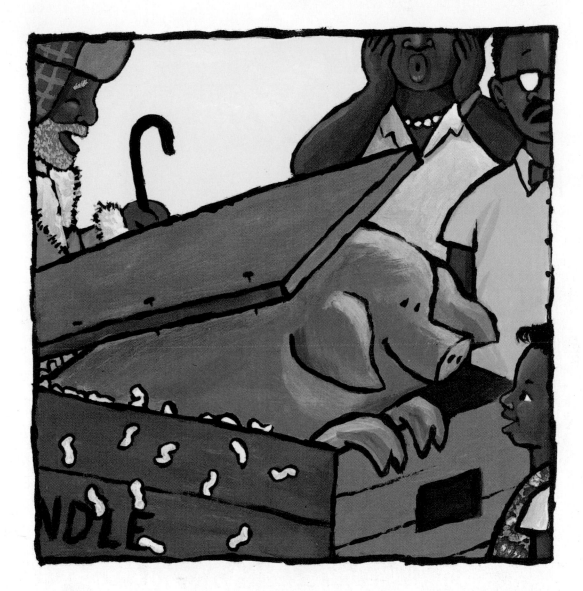

But it was a pig.

A big pig.

An Alaskan pig, who did a polar bear imitation
and climbed out of the crate.

Julius had come.

Maya's parents didn't think that they would like
Julius. He showed them no fun, no sharing.

Maya loved Julius, though, so he stayed.

There never was enough food in the
house after Julius came to stay.
    He slurped coffee and ate too much
peanut butter.

He would roll himself in flour when he wanted
Maya to bake him cookies.

Julius made big messes and spread the
newspaper everywhere before anyone could read it.

He left crumbs on the sheets and never picked
up his towels.

Julius made too much noise. He'd stay up
late watching old movies,

and he'd always play records when everybody
else wanted to read.

But Maya knew the other Julius, too. . . .

The Julius who was fun to take on walks 'cause he did great dog imitations and chased cats.

The Julius who sneaked into stores with her
and tried on clothes. Julius liked anything blue and
stretchy.

They'd try on hats too. Maya liked red
felt. Julius liked straw — it tasted better.

Trying on shoes was hard, though. . . .

Julius would swing for hours on the
playground with Maya.

He'd protect her from the scary things at night
too . . . sometimes.

Maya loved the Julius who taught her how to
dance to jazz records . . .

and eat peanut butter from the jar, without getting any on the ceiling.

Maya didn't think all the older brothers in the world could have taught her that.

Julius loved the Maya who taught him that even though he was a pig he didn't have to act like he lived in a barn.

Julius didn't think all the Alaskan pigs in the
world could have taught him that.

Maya shared the things she'd learned from Julius
with her friends.

Swinging . . .

trying on hats, and dancing to jazz records.

Julius shared the things Maya had taught him with her parents . . . sometimes.

And that was all right, because living with Maya
and sharing everything was even better than being a
cool pig from Alaska.

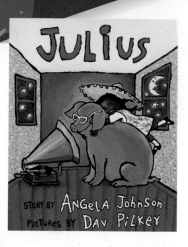

Think About the Selection

1. Why do you think Maya wanted an older brother?

2. How is Julius like most real pigs? How is he not like a real pig?

3. How do you think your family would feel if Julius moved into your home?

4. Why do you think Maya's parents let Julius stay in their home?

5. **Connecting/Comparing** How are Dragon and Julius alike? How are they different?

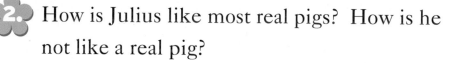

HANDLE WITH CARE

Write a Character Sketch

Choose one of the characters in the story: Maya, Julius, Granddaddy, or one of Maya's parents. Write a description of that character.

Tips

- Remember to include things that the character says and does.
- Use exact nouns, such as *records* or *cookies*.

Reading · Language

Compare story elements (R3.1)
Use parts of speech correctly (LC1.3)

Use a Map or Globe

Find the United States on a map or globe.

- In which state does Granddaddy live? Point it out.

- In which state does Granddaddy spend the winter?

Bonus When Granddaddy goes home for the winter, in which direction does he travel? Explain your answer.

Compare Pictures

Dav Pilkey drew the pictures for both *Dragon Gets By* and *Julius*. With a partner, look at both stories and discuss the pictures.

Tips

- Use two books. Open one to *Julius*. Open the other to *Dragon Gets By*.
- Compare colors, shapes, and backgrounds.

Internet

E-mail a Friend

What did you like best about *Julius*? Would you tell a friend to read it? Send an e-mail to a friend. Tell your friend about the story.

It's Easy to Be Polite

(Why Manners Are Important)

by Beth Brainard and Sheila Behr

The key to being polite is to live by the Golden Rule — treat all people the way you would like them to treat you.

The Magic Words

Thank you!

You're welcome.

Make sure you use the Magic Words every day:

Please
Thank you
You're welcome
Excuse me

Telephone Etiquette

"Hey, Mom, it's for you!"

When you make a call:

Hello, this is Suzi.
May I please speak to Ashley?

- Say *hello*.

- Give your name.

- Ask for the person you're calling. If the person is not there, leave a message or say, *thank you* and *good-bye*. Then hang up. (Always say *good-bye* before hanging up.)

- If you dial a wrong number, say *I'm sorry* and *good-bye*. Then hang up.

When you answer the phone:

- Say *hello*.

- If the caller does not give his or her name, say, "May I ask who's calling?"

- Do not giggle or act silly.

- Never stand by the phone and shout. It is always a good idea to go find the person who is wanted on the phone.

> Mom, there's a phone call for you.

When "Call Waiting" signals:

> Excuse me for just a moment, Ashley. I'll be right back.

> Hello . . . T. J., I'm on the other line. May I call you right back? Thank you. Good-bye.

When leaving a message:

"...at the tone it's a good idea to leave a proper message. BEEP!"

Hello, this is T. J. Jones. I'm calling Suzi. Please call me when you get home. My number is 555-4321. Good-bye.

(T. J. knows how to leave a good message.)

Here are some Phone Tips:

- ◉ Speak clearly.

- ◉ Always use the Magic Words.

- ◉ Do not eat, drink, or chew gum while talking.

- ◉ Always say *good-bye* before hanging up.

- ◉ When someone else is on the line, don't listen. Wait your turn.

Mrs. Brown Went to Town
by Wong Herbert Yee

Life on a Farm

The story you are about to read takes place on a make-believe farm. Life on a real farm is busy. There's a lot of work to do before food from a farm can be **delivered** to stores and markets.

Each morning, cows are **released** into the fields. At night, they return to their barns.

You may see farmers **wearing** gloves or boots. Farm work can be messy.

Feathers fly when it's feeding time in the chicken coop. What a **commotion**!

After a long day, farmers begin to **tire**. They know it's important to rest, because tomorrow will be another busy day.

Meet the Author and Illustrator
Wong Herbert Yee

"My advice to people starting out is that being an artist is not something you do. It's what you are. So stick with it! Find a way."

Fact File

- Wong Herbert Yee was born in Detroit, Michigan.
- He now lives in Troy, Michigan.
- His birthday is August 19.
- He has a wife, Judy, and a daughter, Ellen.
- His hobbies include running and bicycling.
- Mr. Yee remembers wanting to be an artist in first grade. "I can still picture my teacher tacking my drawing of a horse with feedbag on the bulletin board. A proud moment."

Other books by Wong Herbert Yee:

Fireman Small to the Rescue; Eek! There's a Mouse in the House; A Drop of Rain

Internet

To find out more about Wong Herbert Yee, visit Education Place.

www.eduplace.com/kids

Mrs. Brown Went to Town

by Wong Herbert Yee

Use what you know about animals and make-believe to **predict** what might happen on the farm when Mrs. Brown goes to town.

Science Predictions based on patterns (S4.a)

Mrs. Brown lives in the barn out back
With a cow, two pigs, three ducks, and a yak.
Life on the farm wasn't always this way.
Everything changed just last Saturday.

When riding her bicycle down the street,
A terrier tasted Mrs. Brown's feet.

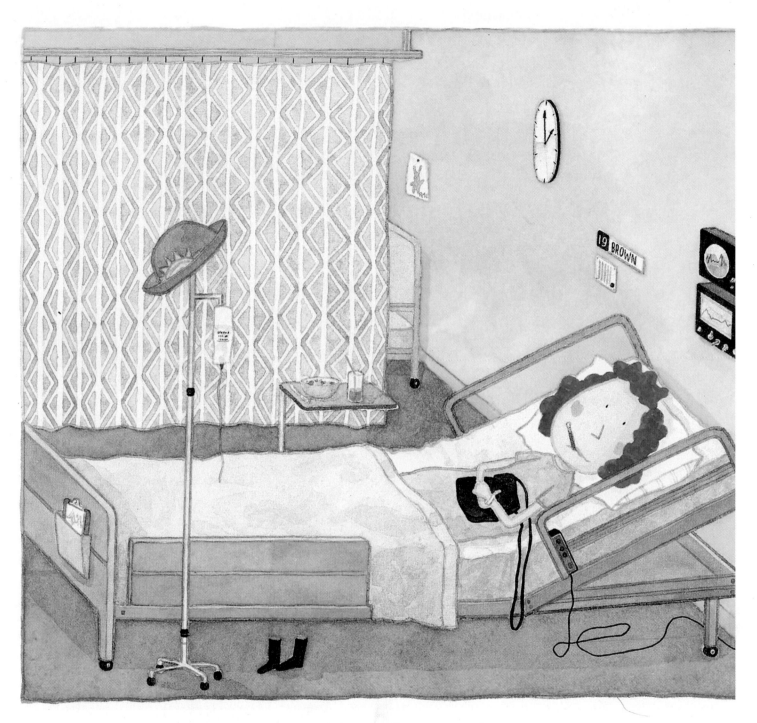

In a hospital bed she rested,
Waiting to be x-rayed and tested.

Mrs. Brown sent word in a letter

To say she'd come home, when she was better.

The postman delivered the letter out back

For a cow, two pigs, three ducks, and a yak.

All the animals, except for a mouse,
Voted to move into Mrs. Brown's house.

They rang the doorbell
To hear the chimes,

Flushed the toilet
One hundred times,

Raced up the stairs, came sliding back down,
Each one wearing a different gown,

Took turns bouncing on Mrs. Brown's bed,

Painted the house in matching barn red.

They raided the pantry,
Prepared a snack
For a cow, two pigs,
Three ducks, and a yak.

95

In the bathroom they played for hours
Putting on makeup and taking long showers.

They dried off in front of a roaring fire,
Warm and cozy but beginning to tire,

Tiptoed upstairs by candlelight,
Borrowed pajamas to wear for the night.

The hospital released Mrs. Brown at eight.
A taxicab dropped her off by the gate.

She hobbled upstairs and crawled in the sack
Didn't see a cow, two pigs, three ducks, and a yak.

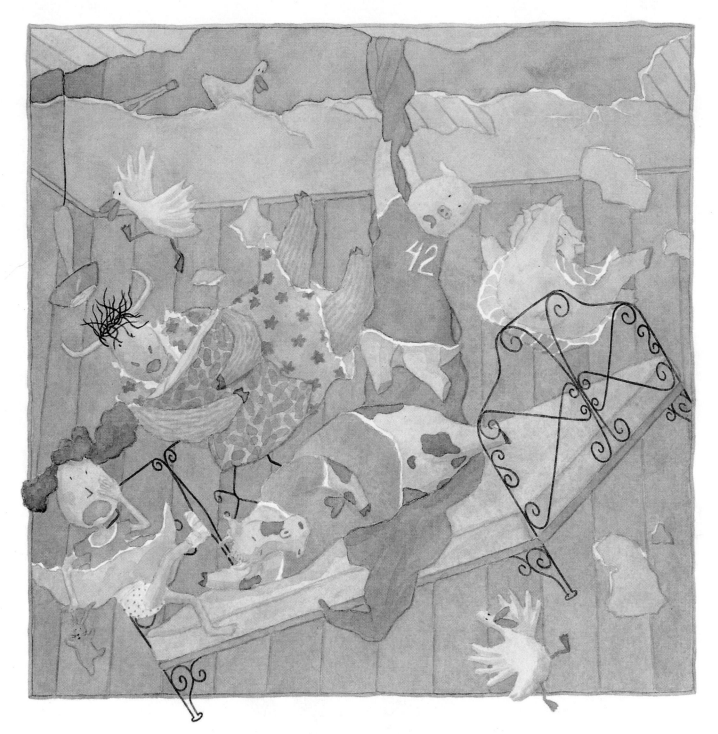

The floor beneath them began to quake.
The walls and windows started to shake.
All this commotion woke Mrs. Brown
In time to feel her bed crashing down!

The police were first to arrive on the scene.
Fire trucks dispatched from station thirteen.

An ambulance raced all the way from town
And carried away poor Mrs. Brown.

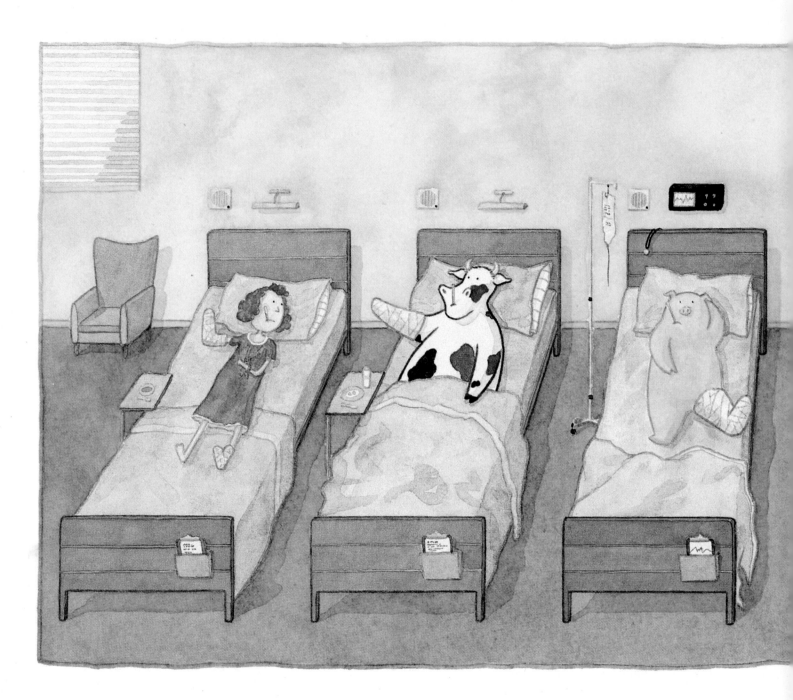

In the hospital she lay on her back
With a cow, two pigs, three ducks, and a yak.

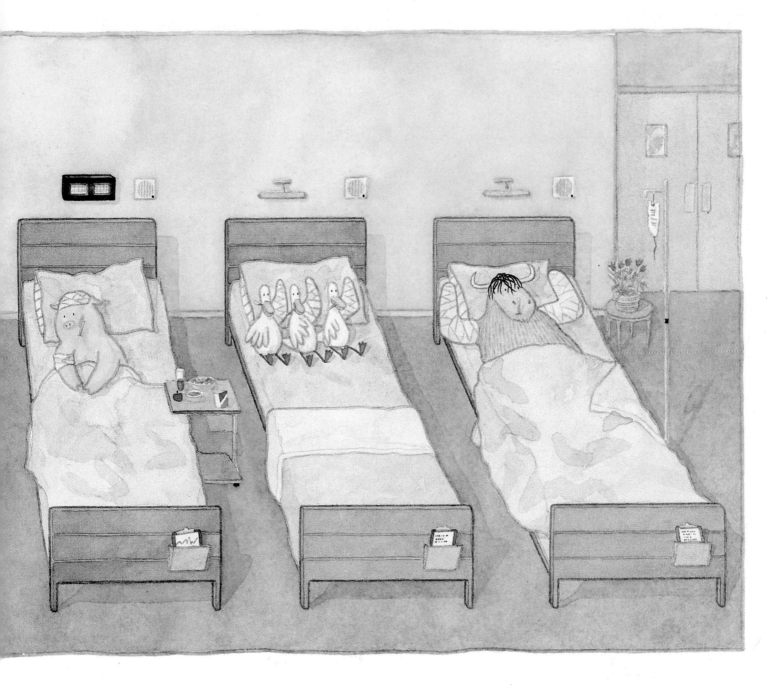

The hospital released Mrs. Brown at ten.
The doctors waved good-bye once again.

Into a taxi they crammed all eight.

The driver dropped them off by the gate.

He swept out the feathers and hair

And charged Mrs. Brown twice the fare.

Life on the farm wasn't always this way
Until Mrs. Brown went to town that day.
So now she lives in the barn out back
With a cow, two pigs, three ducks, and a yak.

Mrs. Brown Went to Town
by Wong Herbert Yee

Think About the Selection

1. Why do you think the animals wanted to move into Mrs. Brown's house?

2. Why didn't the mouse want to move into the house with the other animals?

3. How does Wong Herbert Yee make this story funny? Give examples of funny words and pictures from the story.

4. What do you think life is like for Mrs. Brown now that she lives in the barn?

5. **Connecting/Comparing** What do you think would happen if Mrs. Brown's animals moved in with Maya and Julius?

Creating

Write a Get-Well Card

Cheer up Mrs. Brown while she is in the hospital. Write and illustrate a get-well card for her.

Tips

- For fun, try writing a poem that rhymes.
- Be sure to sign your card.

Reading Impact of alternative endings (R3.2)

Math
Write a Number Sentence

Eight animals voted on whether to move into Mrs. Brown's house. One animal voted not to move into the house. How many animals voted to move into the house? Write a number sentence to solve the problem.

Science
Compare Animals

Copy the chart below on a piece of paper. What body parts does each animal have? Put check marks where they belong.

	Wings	Horns	Feathers	Tail
Cow				
Yak				
Duck				
Pig				

Internet
Send an E-postcard

Did you like reading the books in this theme? If you want to tell a friend about these books, send an e-postcard. You'll find one at Education Place.

www.eduplace.com/kids

Oodles of Riddles

1

Why should you not tell pigs secrets?

Because pigs are squealers.

Blab!   Blab!

2

What do you call a cow wearing a crown?

A dairy queen.

3

Where do sheep get their hair cut?

At the baa-baa shop.

4

Where do cows go on dates?

To the moo-vies.

5

Why did the duck cross the road?

The chicken was on vacation.

6

What did the cow wear on a cruise?

A moomoo.

111

✔ Choosing the Best Answer

Some tests have questions with three or four answer choices. How do you choose the best answer? Look at this sample test question for *Julius*. The correct answer is shown. Use the tips to help you answer this kind of test question.

Tips

- Read the directions carefully.
- Read the question and all the answer choices.
- Look back at the selection if you need to.
- Fill in the answer circle completely.

Read the question. Fill in the circle next to the best answer.

1 Which of the following could really happen?

○ A pig can play records and dance.

● A pig can make noise.

○ A pig can swing on a playground swing.

Reading
State purpose in reading (R2.2)
Follow written instructions (R2.8)

Now see how one student figured out the best answer.

I am looking for the answer that tells what could happen in **real life**. All of the answer choices tell about something that happened in the story.

I read the answer choices again. The first and third answers could not happen in real life. Now I see why the second answer is the best choice.

Nature Walk

I'm Glad

I'm glad the sky is painted blue,

And the earth is painted green,

With such a lot of nice fresh air

All sandwiched in between.

Anonymous

Nature Walk

Contents

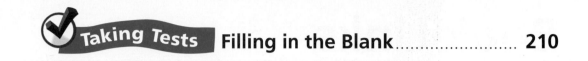

Phonics Library

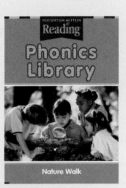

- Miss Pig's Garden
- Mike and Dave Sleep Outside
- A Trip to Central Park
- Zeke and Pete Rule!
- In the Woods
- A Snake Sheds Its Skin

Big Book

Time to Sleep
by Denise Fleming

Theme Paperbacks

Amelia Bedelia Goes Camping
by Peggy Parish

Chibi
by Barbara Brenner and Julia Takaya

On My Way Practice Reader

Animal Tracks Are Everywhere
by Misha Millarky

Book Links

If you like . . .

Henry and Mudge and the Starry Night
by Cynthia Rylant

Then try . . .

Henry and Mudge and the Wild Wind

by Cynthia Rylant
(Aladdin)

During a booming thunderstorm, Henry and Mudge keep busy indoors.

Secret Place

by Eve Bunting
(Clarion)

A boy finds a place in the city where ducks nest and possums come to drink.

If you like . . .

Exploring Parks with Ranger Dockett
by Alice K. Flanagan

Then try . . .

Riding the Ferry with Captain Cruz

by Alice K. Flanagan
(Children's Press)

Captain Cruz takes people back and forth from Staten Island to New York City.

Pink Snow and Other Weird Weather

by Jennifer Dussling
(Grosset)

Pink snow? Toads falling from the sky? Learn about these and other weird weather facts.

If you like . . .

Around the Pond: Who's Been Here?

by Lindsay Barrett George

Then try . . .

In the Woods: Who's Been Here?

by Lindsay Barrett George
(Greenwillow)

During a walk, a boy and girl find clues about which animals live in the woods.

Bugs! Bugs! Bugs!

by Jennifer Dussling
(DK)

Fierce insects hunt and trick their enemies to stay alive.

Technology

At Education Place

Post your reviews of these books or see what others had to say.

Education Place®
www.eduplace.com/kids

. . .

At school

Read at school and take a quiz.

Accelerated Reader®

. . .

At home

Read at home and log on to

Book Adventure™

www.bookadventure.org

HENRY AND MUDGE
AND THE
Starry Night

Story by Cynthia Rylant
Pictures by Suçie Stevenson

California Standards

Standards to Achieve

Reading

• **Meaning of compound words (R1.8)**

120

Camping and Hiking

In the story you are going to read, a family goes camping and hiking. Have you ever gone **camping** in the woods? Have you ever **climbed** a hill? Spending time outdoors can be a lot of fun.

◀ You can carry what you need in a **backpack**.

▶ You can cook over a **campfire**.

▲ A **tent** protects you from rain, wind, or hot sunshine.

▼ A **lantern** is a light you can use outdoors.

Meet the Author
Cynthia Rylant

Where she lives: Eugene, Oregon

How she got the idea for Henry and Mudge: When her son was seven, they met a "big, drooly dog" named Mudge.

Fun fact: Her dog Leia is pictured in Dav Pilkey's book, *Dogzilla*.

Other books by Cynthia Rylant:
Mr. Putter and Tabby Toot the Horn
Poppleton and Friends
The Relatives Came

Meet the Illustrator
Suçie Stevenson

Where she lives: By the sea on Cape Cod in Massachusetts

Pets: She has two Labrador retriever dogs that sleep under her desk while she works. If she ever forgets how Mudge would act, she just looks under her desk.

Internet

To find out more about Cynthia Rylant and Suçie Stevenson, visit Education Place.

www.eduplace.com/kids

122

HENRY AND MUDGE
AND THE
Starry Night

Story by Cynthia Rylant
Pictures by Suçie Stevenson

Henry and Mudge find a lot to do while they are camping. As you read, think of **questions** that you might ask about their camping trip.

Big Bear Lake

In August Henry and Henry's big dog Mudge
always went camping. They went with Henry's
parents.

Henry's mother had been a Camp Fire Girl, so she knew all about camping. She knew how to set up a tent. She knew how to build a campfire. She knew how to cook camp food.

Henry's dad didn't know anything about camping.
He just came with a guitar and a smile.

Henry and Mudge loved camping. This year they
were going to Big Bear Lake, and Henry couldn't wait.

"We'll see deer, Mudge," Henry said. Mudge wagged.

"We'll see raccoons," said Henry. Mudge shook Henry's hand.

"We might even see a *bear*," Henry said.

Henry was not so sure he wanted to see a bear. He shivered and put an arm around Mudge.

Mudge gave a big, slow, *loud* yawn. He drooled on Henry's foot.

Henry giggled. "No bear will get *us*, Mudge," Henry said. "We're too *slippery*!"

A Good Smelly Hike

Henry and Mudge and Henry's parents drove
to Big Bear Lake. They parked the car and got
ready to hike.

Everyone had a backpack, even Mudge. (His
had lots of crackers.)

Henry's mother said, "Let's go!" And off
they went.

They walked and walked and climbed and
climbed. It was beautiful.

Henry saw a fish jump straight out of a stream. He saw a doe and her fawn. He saw waterfalls and a rainbow.

Mudge didn't see much of anything. He was
smelling. Mudge loved to hike and smell.

He smelled a raccoon from yesterday. He
smelled a deer from last night. He smelled an
oatmeal cookie from Henry's back pocket.

"Mudge!" Henry laughed, giving Mudge
the cookie.

Finally Henry's mother picked a good place to camp.
Henry's parents set up the tent. Henry unpacked
the food and pans and lanterns. Mudge unpacked a
ham sandwich.

136

Finally the camp was almost ready. It needed just one more thing:

"Who knows the words to 'Love Me Tender'?" said Henry's father with a smile, pulling out his guitar. Henry looked at Mudge and groaned.

Green Dreams

It was a beautiful night. Henry and Henry's parents lay on their backs by the fire and looked at the sky.

Henry didn't know there were so many stars in the sky.

"There's the Big Dipper," said Henry's mother.

"There's the Little Dipper," said Henry.

"There's E. T.," said Henry's dad.

Mudge wasn't looking at stars. He was chewing on a log. He couldn't get logs this good at home. Mudge loved camping.

Henry's father sang one more sappy
love song, then everyone went inside the
tent to sleep.

Henry's father and mother snuggled. Henry
and Mudge snuggled.

It was as quiet as quiet could be. Everyone slept safe and sound and there were no bears, no scares. Just the clean smell of trees . . . and wonderful green dreams.

Responding

Think About the Selection

1. Why does Henry love camping? Why does Mudge love camping?

2. What might have happened if the family had seen a bear while camping?

3. Is it a good idea to take a dog on a camping trip? Explain.

4. What would have been different about Henry's trip if it had rained the whole time?

5. **Connecting/Comparing** If you were to go on a nature walk with Henry and Mudge, what would you enjoy most?

Reflecting

Write a Journal Entry

Choose a character from the story: Henry, his mom or dad, or even Mudge. Write a journal entry about the camping trip from that character's point of view.

Tips

- Make a list of what took place on the trip.
- Tell what happened first, next, and last.

Reading Cause-and-effect relationships (R2.6)
Impact of alternative endings (R3.2)

Make a Map

Henry saw hills and other land forms while hiking. Draw a map of Big Bear Lake. Label some of the land forms Henry saw.

Bonus **Write a short description of each land form.**

Make a Camping Catalog

Make a catalog of things campers use. Draw or cut out pictures of items such as a tent or a backpack. Then, label each picture.

Internet

Do a Web Mystery Grid

To find a surprise from the camping trip, print a mystery grid from Education Place.

www.eduplace.com/kids

Writing Organize related ideas (W1.1)

Social Studies Link

Skill: How to Read Instructions

❶ Read the title.

❷ Read through all of the instructions.

❸ Study the pictures or diagrams.

❹ Look for clue words such as *then, while,* or *until.*

❺ Reread the instructions carefully.

California Standards

Standards to Achieve

Reading

• Use expository text features (R2.1)

• Information from visuals (R2.7)

150

CAMPFIRE GAMES

by Jane Drake and Ann Love

OFFICIAL BOOK OF CAMPFIRE FUN · BUILD A FIRE · SING SONGS · PLAY GAMES

THE KIDS CAMPFIRE BOOK

GHOST STORIES · NATURE · RECIPES

WRITTEN BY JANE DRAKE & ANN LOVE
ILLUSTRATED BY HEATHER COLLINS

· HUNDREDS OF FUN THINGS TO DO ·

Telephone

Everyone sits in a circle around or near the fire. One person starts the game by whispering a message in the ear of the person on her right. She might say a tongue twister or something simple, such as "Dad cooks great burgers" or "Mary mixes marvelous milk shakes."

The message is passed from ear to ear until the last person repeats what he's been told. You'll be in stitches when you hear "Cool Dad eats bridges" or "Mash mealy muffins, Mary."

Campfire Telephone

Everyone sitting in the campfire circle joins hands. The person with a birthday closest to July 1 starts the game by squeezing a message to the person seated on his right. It can be an ordinary squeeze, or a series of squeezes like Morse code.

The message travels around the circle until it comes back to the start. See how much the message changes. Try to do it quickly so that the message flashes around the circle in the shortest time possible.

Rainmaker

If it's been a hot day and you need cooling off, try rainmaking. One person begins and is joined by the person on her right and so on until the action travels all the way around the circle.

The noise gets louder as each person in the circle joins in. Then the first person will do the next action and it will travel around the circle.

Round 1

Rub your hands together so they make a swishing noise.

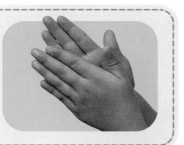

Round 2

Snap the fingers of both hands, moving your arms up and down, while making a popping sound with your tongue on the roof of your mouth. It sounds like water falling to the ground.

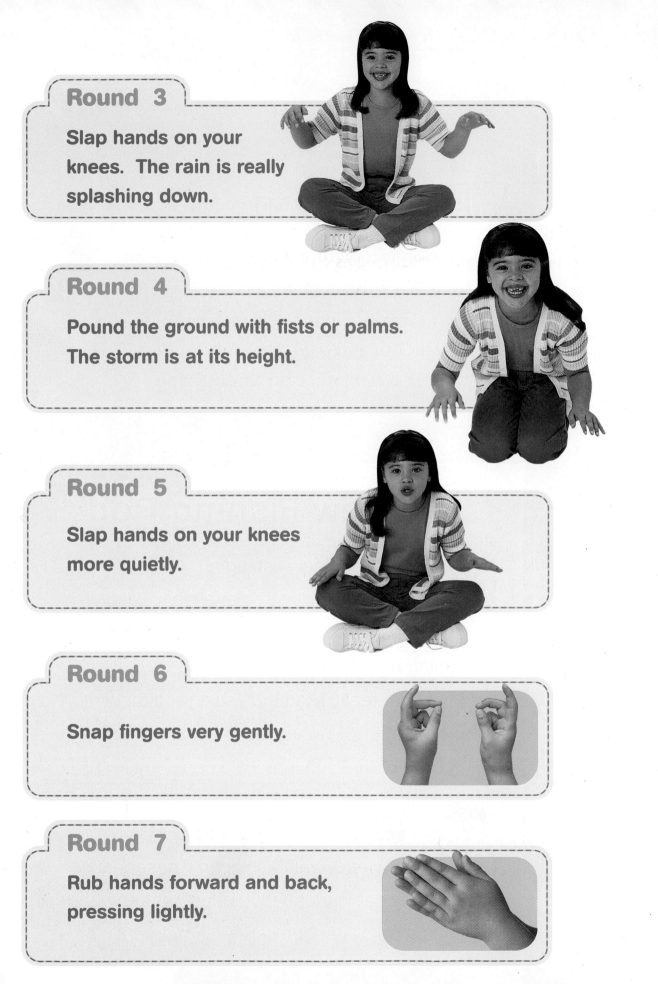

Round 3

Slap hands on your knees. The rain is really splashing down.

Round 4

Pound the ground with fists or palms. The storm is at its height.

Round 5

Slap hands on your knees more quietly.

Round 6

Snap fingers very gently.

Round 7

Rub hands forward and back, pressing lightly.

A Description

A description is a picture in words that helps the reader to see, hear, taste, feel, and smell what you're writing about. Use this student's writing as a model when you write a story of your own.

My New Fishing Rod

I bought a new fishing rod that I haven't used yet. It is red and black with white string and a black handle. I got my fishing rod at the mall and paid $11.99 for it. My father really liked the fishing rod that I picked out. It is in my dad's car in the trunk in back of the car where I'll keep it until summer. Then I can use it a lot.

I caught three fish one day last summer when I went fishing in Chesapeake Bay. My dad caught a flounder, and then he caught an oyster cracker. A flounder is as

> A good **beginning** tells what the description is about.

> A good description includes **sense words**.

Writing — Write brief narratives (W2.1)
Write a description (W2.1.b)

flat as a stone. The oyster cracker that my dad caught was covered with spots. I couldn't believe how ugly it was!

After fishing, we took the fish home, cleaned them, and then we ate them. Once we finished eating the fish, we went to bed. We had a fantastic time fishing.

I cannot wait to use my new fishing rod. I'll be glad when it is hot. Then I can go fishing and catch all kinds of fish like catfish, rockfish, perch, and flounder.

Telling what happened is a good way to make a description interesting to the reader.

Giving **specific names** for what you've been describing makes a good ending.

Meet the Author

Robert C.

Grade: two

State: Delaware

Hobbies: reading, Boy Scouts, fishing

What he'd like to be when he grows up: worker in the field of marine wildlife

Exploring Parks with Ranger Dockett

written by
ALICE K. FLANAGAN

photographs by
CHRISTINE OSINSKI

California Standards

Standards to Achieve

Reading

• Author's purpose (R2.3)

Park Rangers

What does a park **ranger** do? Rangers care for and **protect** the plants and animals in their parks. They teach people about nature.

There are different kinds of rangers. Some are **urban** rangers who work in city parks. Others work in forests and national parks.

In the next selection, you'll learn more about what rangers do.

Rangers greet **visitors** to the park.

Rangers give **tours** of the park.

Often, rangers help animals in their own **habitat**.

Rangers show people the animals in the park.

Exploring nature with children is a fun part of the job.

Author
Alice K. Flanagan

Photographer
Christine Osinski

Meet the Author and the Photographer

Alice Flanagan and Christine Osinski are sisters. They grew up in Chicago, Illinois. When they were children, they would make books together by writing stories and drawing pictures.

Today, they still team up to make books. Ms. Flanagan writes the words and Ms. Osinski takes the photos.

Other books:

A Busy Day at Mr. Kang's Grocery Store

Dr. Kanner, Dentist with a Smile

Here Comes Mr. Eventoff with the Mail!

Internet

Visit Education Place to find out more about Alice Flanagan and Christine Osinski.

www.eduplace.com/kids

158

Selection 2

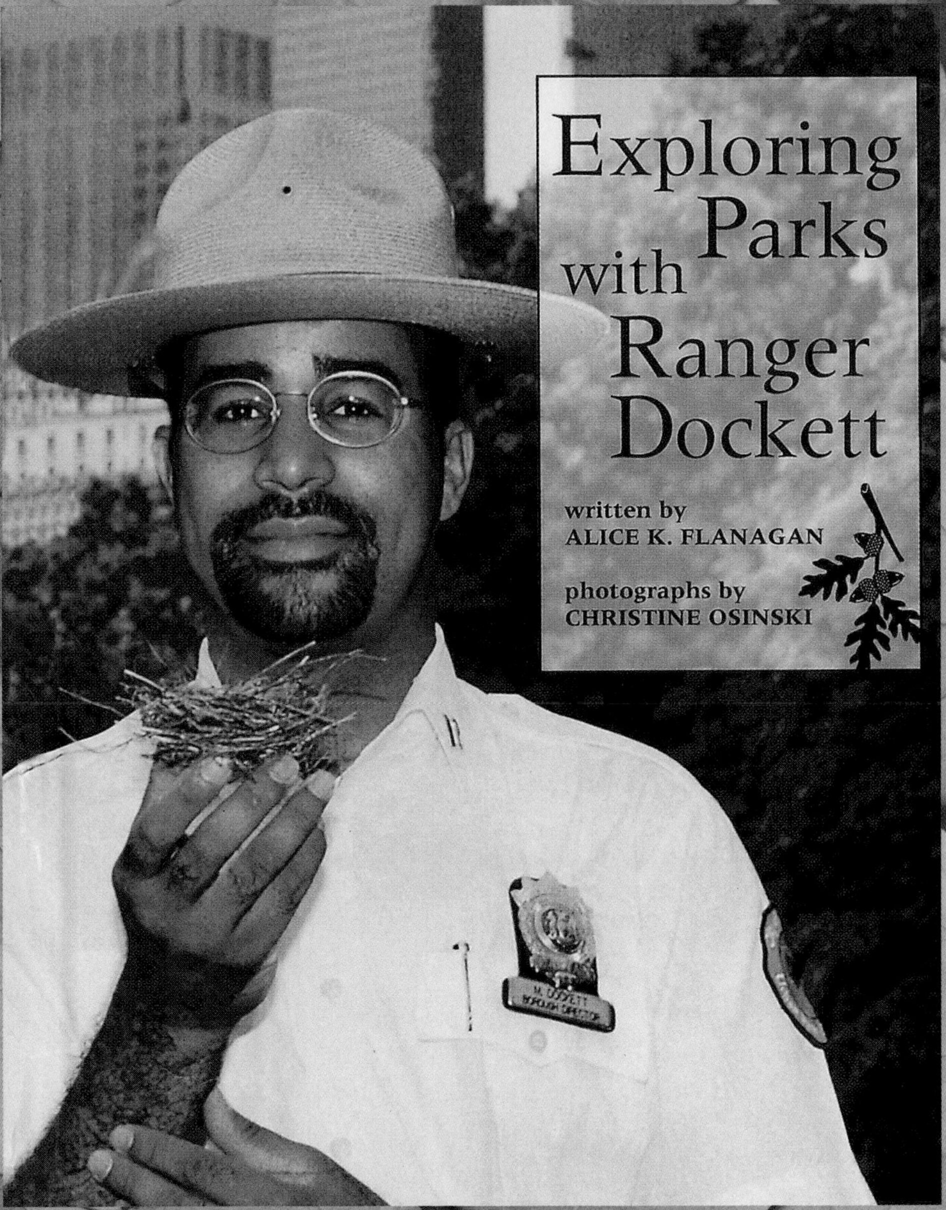
Exploring Parks with Ranger Dockett
written by
ALICE K. FLANAGAN
photographs by
CHRISTINE OSINSKI

Strategy Focus

Ranger Dockett has a busy job. As you read the selection, **evaluate** how the author helps you understand what rangers do.

Right in the middle of busy New York City is a wide, wonderful park.

It is one of many parks that Ranger Dockett takes care of as an Urban Park Ranger.

Each day, he has many tasks. He takes visitors on bird-watching walks. And he gives special tours of the parks.

Sometimes, he talks about the statues
along the paths.

There's Christopher Columbus and Alice
in Wonderland with the Mad Hatter!

On his long walks through the city parks, Ranger Dockett keeps in touch with other rangers.

Together, they make sure everyone follows the rules to keep the parks safe and clean.

Ranger Dockett does his best to make each park a safe place where people can walk or play.

Every day, Ranger Dockett teaches people how to care for the special green spaces in the heart of the city. He shows them how to protect the plants and animals that live there.

Each year, he plants young trees. He explains
how important they are to the park habitat.

Sometimes, he teaches classes at the pond. He talks about the plant life at the water's edge.

His students look for turtles, frogs, and insects.

Ranger Dockett puts on special boots.
Carefully, he wades to the middle of the pond
with his net.

When he brings back mud from the bottom
of the pond, everyone searches for signs of life.
Will they find a beetle or a dragonfly?

Look! There's a snail!

Ranger Dockett was a Boy Scout when
he was a little boy. Later, he went to school
to learn how to be a ranger.

Ever since then, he has been exploring
nature with others.

The park is his exciting classroom!

Responding

Think About the Selection

1. What did you learn about Ranger Dockett's busy job?

2. If you were a park ranger, what part of the job would you like best? Why?

3. Why is a park ranger's job important?

4. In what ways is a park like an exciting classroom?

5. **Connecting/Comparing** If Henry and Mudge were to visit Ranger Dockett's park, what would their day be like?

Informing

Write Park Rules

Ranger Dockett makes sure that everyone follows park rules. Write a list of rules for Ranger Dockett's park.

Tips

- Use command sentences, such as *Obey park rules.*
- Use words such as *always* or *never.*

Reading
Language

Questions about expository text (R2.4)
Use correct word order (LC1.2)

Math

Make a Schedule

Write a list of what Ranger Dockett does in one day. Then write a time for when he might begin and end each task. Put the times in order.

Bonus Use a calculator to add the minutes for each task. Find the total number of minutes.

Listening and Speaking

Give a Talk

Role-play a visit from Ranger Dockett to your class. Plan his talk with a small group. Choose group members to be the teacher, Ranger Dockett, and the audience.

> **Tips**
> - Take turns speaking.
> - Speak clearly in a voice that can be heard.

Go on a Web Field Trip

Connect to Education Place and explore a national park or wildlife preserve.

www.eduplace.com/kids

Math
Listening/Speaking
Time/time relationships (MMG1.4)
Speak clearly/appropriately (LS1.6)

175

Oak's Introduction

I've been wondering,
when you'd notice
me standing here.

I've been waiting,
watching you
grow taller.

I have grown too.
My branches
are strong.

Step closer.
Let's see
how high

you can

climb.

by Kristine O'Connell George

Looking Around

Bees
    own the clover,
birds
    own the sky,
rabbits,
    the meadow
    with low grass and high.

Frogs
    own the marshes,
ants
    own the ground . . .
    I hope they don't mind
    my looking around.

by Aileen Fisher

177

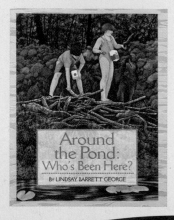

Around the Pond: Who's Been Here?
BY LINDSAY BARRETT GEORGE

Ponds

A pond is a body of water, smaller than a lake. In the next story, two children find many interesting animals and plants in and around a pond.

A **path** near a pond may have been made by the footsteps of animals or people.

Some fish make a small **crater** in the soil under the water to lay their eggs.

The water near the **edge** of a pond is usually not deep.

Moss and other green plants grow near the water's edge, on the **banks** of the pond.

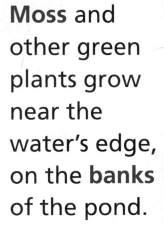

Sometimes it is possible to see small fish and other living things in **shallow** water.

Meet the Author and Illustrator

Lindsay Barrett George

Birthday: July 22

Where she was born:
The Dominican Republic

Where she lives now:
She lives in a log cabin in
Pennsylvania with her
husband and her children,
William and Campbell.

Why she wrote this book:
She spent four years living
with her family in their home
near the woods. She thought
children would enjoy reading
about the animals that were
her neighbors.

Other books:

In the Snow: Who's Been Here?
*Around the World: Who's
Been Here?*

Internet

To find out more about Lindsay Barrett George, visit
Education Place.

www.eduplace.com/kids

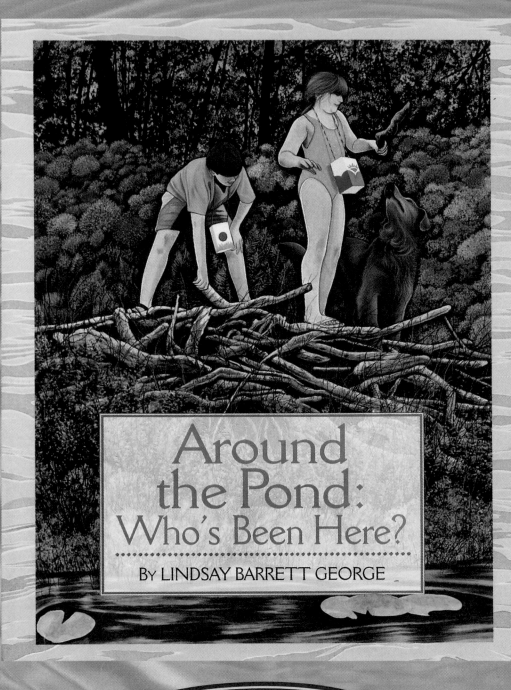

Around the Pond: Who's Been Here?

By LINDSAY BARRETT GEORGE

As you read about Cammy and William's trip around the pond, **monitor** your reading. If you don't understand something, reread to **clarify** what happened.

It is warm and muggy on this summer afternoon.

"Cammy," says William, "Mom says if we pick enough blueberries, we can make a pie for dinner."

"Let's go!" says Cammy.

Cammy and her brother grab their berry containers and follow the old deer path that circles the pond.

A dead sugar maple stands alone by the water's edge.

White feathers are stuck to the bark around a hole.

Who's been here?

Two baby wood ducks

Sam finds a stick. He wants someone to throw it.

"Not now, Sam," William says. "We've got to pick blueberries."

Their dog lies down on the soft sphagnum moss.

"William, look at this footprint," says Cammy.

Who's been here?

A baby raccoon

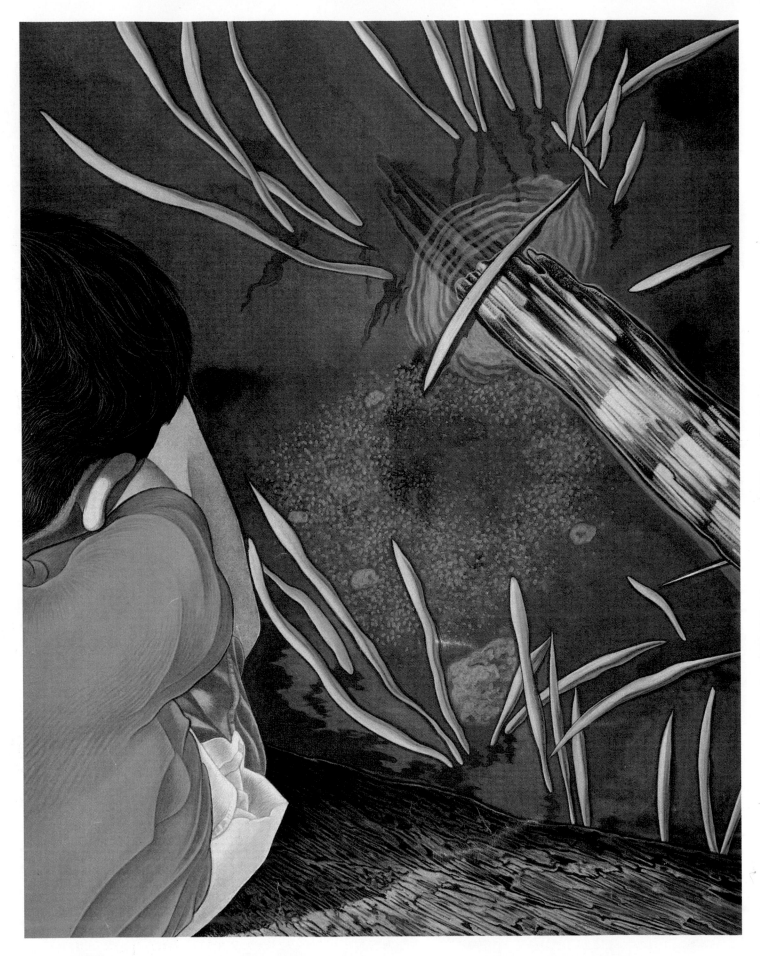

A tree has fallen across the path and into the pond.

William dangles his feet in the water. He sees a shallow crater on the sandy bottom.

Who's been here?

A sunfish

Cammy and William reach a patch
of swamp azalea. They see a pile of
branches and mud.

Who's been here?

A beaver

Bits of broken shell lie on the sunny bank. The children stop to take a closer look.

William picks up a piece of shell. It is soft.

Who's been here?

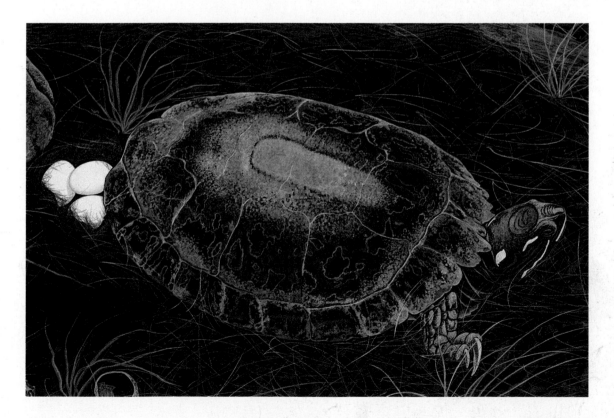

A painted terrapin

Cammy and her brother stop in front of a large blueberry bush. They pick and eat. Sam likes blueberries, too.

Cammy points to a long, filmy shape caught on the branches.

Who's been here?

A garter snake

Sam wades into the pond and takes a drink.

A red-winged blackbird scolds from a nearby branch. A large, gray feather floats next to a lily pad.

Who's been here?

A great blue heron

198

The pond is quiet and still. The late afternoon sky turns pink.

"Let's go wading," says Cammy. The mud is soft and squishy.

"Look at all the mussel shells," says William.

Who's been here?

An otter

Cammy and William reach the dock.
They have eaten most of their blueberries.
But look! Two full pails of berries are
waiting for them.

Who's been here? They know!

"Come and join us,"
calls their father.
And in they go!

Responding

Around the Pond: Who's Been Here?
BY LINDSAY BARRETT GEORGE

Think About the Selection

1. Think about the animals in this story. In what ways are they alike? How are they different?

2. Cammy and William are good nature detectives. What do you think makes a good nature detective?

3. How would this story be different if it took place in winter?

4. If Cammy and William visited Ranger Dockett's park, what clues might they find there?

5. **Connecting/Comparing** Compare Sam, the dog in this story, with Mudge. How are they alike?

Describing

Describe an Animal

Choose a picture of an animal from the story. Write a description of that animal.

Tips

- List details about the animal.
- Use adjectives to describe how the animal looks, smells, and feels.

Reading

Compare story elements (R3.1)
Impact of alternative endings (R3.2)

Identify Living Things

Make a chart with three columns. Label one column **L** for *Living*. Label the second column **N** for *Non-living*. Label the third column **O** for *Once-living*. Then look at the story and group things that you find.

Look for Classroom Clues

Practice being a detective in your classroom or school. Look for clues, such as a half-eaten sandwich or a broken crayon. Ask yourself, "Who's been here?"

Tips

- Choose an area of the school or classroom to explore.
- Take notes on what you see.

Internet

Do a Web Crossword Puzzle

Test what you know about the plants and animals in *Around the Pond: Who's Been Here?* Print a crossword puzzle from Education Place.

www.eduplace.com/kids

Reading
Science

Information from visuals (R2.7)
Compare/sort common objects (S4.c)

Science Link

Skill: How to Read a Science Article

❶ **Read** the title, headings, and captions.

❷ **Look** at the pictures or photos.

❸ **Predict** what you will learn.

❹ **Carefully read** the whole article.

California Standards

Standards to Achieve

Reading

• **Use expository text features (R2.1)**

Science

• **Use magnifiers or microscopes (S4.f)**

How to Be a Wildlife Spy

From *Ranger Rick* magazine

by Carolyn Duckworth

Watching wildlife is like a sport — the more you learn and practice, the better you get at it, and the more fun you have!

Look Here, Look There

One of the neat things about spying on wildlife is that you can do it almost anywhere. Even in a car, you can look out the window and try to see hawks soaring in the sky or deer at the edge of woods.

Try Different Times

Deer, birds, and other animals are most active around sunrise and sunset. But lots of creatures are very busy in the middle of the day. At night, *look* for bats and moths and *listen* for all kinds of animals.

Think Small

You can look for insects everywhere. Examine plants closely, peek under dead tree bark, and look in streams and ponds. (Be sure to watch out for stingers and biters.)

squirrel

salamander

hawk

Use All Your Senses

Look around, but also remember to sniff and listen. For example, a musky odor may be the scent of a fox. And honking cries overhead may be a flock of Canada geese.

Check Animal Signs

Sometimes you can figure out where an animal has been or what it has been doing by the signs it has left. Look along a creek for the tracks of birds, beavers, and other animals. And look for places where the grass has been pressed against the ground. A deer may have rested there.

deer track

Let Someone Know

Always let an adult know where you're going and when you'll be back. Or take an adult along — adults like to have fun too.

What to Take

Powerful "eyes." Take a magnifying glass and binoculars if you have them.

Outdoor Manners

There are nice ways and not-so-nice ways to watch wildlife. Remember, you're a guest in the animals' wild homes.

▶ Leave your pets and radio at home.

▶ Don't chase animals or try to make them fly or run. And be careful not to bother them by getting too close.

Filling in the Blank

Some tests use sentences with a blank in them. You must decide which answer choice best fills in each blank. How do you choose the best answer? Look at this sample test sentence for *Around the Pond: Who's Been Here?* The correct answer is shown. Use the tips to help you complete this kind of test sentence.

Tips

- Read the directions carefully.
- Read the sentence to yourself, using each answer choice to fill in the blank.
- Look back at the selection if you need to.
- Fill in the answer circle completely.

Read the sentence. Fill in the circle next to the best answer.

1 Cammy and William saw animal signs such as _____.

- ○ a pail of berries
- ○ the sandy bottom of the pond
- ● bits of broken shell
- ○ a hole in a tree

Reading **Follow written instructions (R2.8)**

Now see how one student figured out the best answer.

How do I choose the best answer to fill in the blank? I am looking for the answer choice that gives an example of an animal sign.

I remember from the story that an animal sign is a clue left by an animal. The first two answer choices do not tell about clues left by animals.

The fourth choice is close but doesn't tell enough. Only the third choice talks about animal signs. Now I see why the third answer choice is correct.

Fables

What can you learn from a story?
Plenty, especially if it's a fable.

What is a fable?

- A fable is a short story that teaches a lesson.
- In fables, the characters are often animals that act and talk like people.
- Fables usually end with a *moral*, or statement that sums up the lesson of the story.

Contents

    From *More Fables of Aesop*
    Retold by Jack Kent

The Hare
and the Tortoise

The hare teased the tortoise about being so pokey.

"I get where I'm going as surely as YOU do!" said the tortoise.

"But I get where I'm going FASTER," said the hare.

The fox suggested they run a race to settle the argument.

The hare laughed so hard at the idea that it made the tortoise angry. "I'll race you and I'll WIN!" the tortoise said.

The race had hardly begun before the speedy hare was out of sight.

The hare was so sure of himself that he lay down by the side of the path to take a short nap. The tortoise kept plodding slowly along.

The hare woke up just in time to see the tortoise cross the finish line and win the race.

Slow and steady wins the race.

The Crow and the Pitcher

A thirsty crow found a pitcher with a little water in the bottom. But he couldn't reach it.

He collected a number of pebbles.

Then he dropped them one by one into the pitcher. Each pebble raised the water a little higher.

And at last the crow could reach it and get a drink.

Little by little does the job.

The Grasshopper and the Ants

All summer long, the grasshopper sat in the sunshine and sang, while the ants were busily gathering food for the winter.

Winter came and the hungry grasshopper asked the ants for a bite to eat.

But the ants sent him away, saying, "If you were foolish enough to sing all the summer, you must dance supperless to bed in the winter."

You can't play all the time.

Belling the Cat

The mice held a meeting to decide what to do to protect themselves from the cat.

One mouse suggested that they tie a bell around his neck so they could hear him coming.

"Belling the cat is a good idea," one old mouse said . . . "but which of us is going to do it?"

Some things are easier said than done.

The Fly on the Wagon

A farm wagon rumbled down a dirt road, stirring up clouds of dust.

A fly that was sitting in the back of the wagon said, "My, my! We're raising a lot of dust, aren't we?"

We sometimes take credit for
more than we do.

Creating

Write a Fable

Think of a lesson that people can use in school or in their everyday lives. Your lesson can be a simple statement that talks about working hard, being fair, or even just telling the truth.

Read several fables to get an idea of how the story helps to explain the lesson. Then write your own fable.

Tips

- **Write a title that will get a reader's attention.**
- **List the animals and objects that will appear in your fable.**
- **Think of a moral for your fable, or choose one from the examples given.**

Morals

Little friends may become great friends.

No one believes liars, even when they tell the truth.

It's easy to dislike what you can't have.

Reading   Compare story versions (R3.3)

Other Collections of Fables

Two Mice in Three Fables

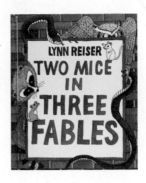

by Lynn Reiser (Greenwillow)
Two mice friends outwit an owl, a raccoon,
and a snake.

Once in a Wood: Ten Tales from Aesop

by Eve Rice (Greenwillow)
Ten simple retellings of fables by Aesop include
"The Lion and the Mouse."

Seven Blind Mice

by Ed Young (Philomel)
In a fable from India, seven mice visit
an elephant.

A Sip of Aesop

by Jane Yolen (Scholastic)
Thirteen of Aesop's fables are retold
as poems.

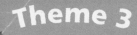

Around Town

Neighborhood and Community

A Neighborhood Is a Friendly Place

A neighborhood is
a friendly place.
A neighborhood is
a friendly place.
You can say hi
to friends passing by.
A neighborhood is
a friendly place.

by Ella Jenkins

226

Around Town:
Neighborhood and Community

Contents

Phonics Library

- **Sunshine for the Circus**
- **Mother's Day Parade on Park Street**
- **Jay the Mailman**
- **Watch Out for Thick Mud!**
- **Mouse's Crowded House**
- **Hooray for Main Street**
- **The Clean Team**
- **Big Hound's Lunch**

Big Book

The Adventures of Taxi Dog
by Debra and Sal Barracca

Theme Paperbacks

Harry's Pony
by Barbara Ann Porte

Solo Girl by Andrea Davis Pinkney

On My Way Practice Reader

Catching Bailey by Becky Cheston

Book Links

If you like . . .

Chinatown
by William Low

Then try . . .

The Ugly Vegetables

by Grace Lin (Charlesbridge)
Can ugly vegetables make a delicious soup? One girl's neighbors think so.

Rush Hour

by Christine Loomis (Houghton)
Where are all the people going? Why are they in such a hurry?

If you like . . .

A Trip to the Firehouse
by Wendy C. Lewison

Then try . . .

Fire Fighter!

by Angela Royston (DK)
Somewhere there's a fire, and firefighters are off to fight it.

Firehorse Max

by Sara London (Harper)
Old Max the horse just can't stand still whenever he hears a fire bell.

Big Bushy Mustache

by Gary Soto

Jamaica Louise James

by Amy Hest

Then try . . .

Then try . . .

Roxaboxen

by *Alice Mclerran* (Puffin)
A rocky hill becomes an imaginary town for Marion and her friends.

The Paperboy

by *Dav Pilkey* (Orchard)
A boy and his dog enjoy delivering newspapers together.

City Green

by *DyAnne DiSalvo-Ryan* (Morrow)
Marcy heads up a project to turn an empty lot into a community garden.

The Little Painter of Sabana Grande

by *P. M. Markun* (Simon)
Fernando makes his village beautiful by painting its walls.

What Is a Chinatown?

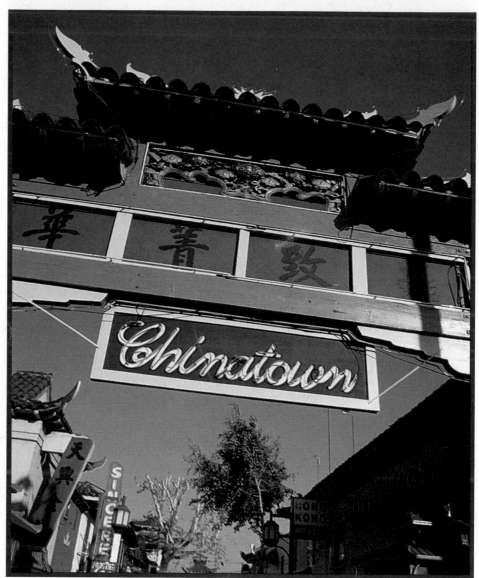

Chinatown is a name used to describe a neighborhood found in some big cities, such as New York City. Many of the people who live and work in Chinatown are Chinese Americans. You'll find out more about Chinatown in the story you're going to read next.

Chinatowns are busy places filled with **apartment** buildings, shops, **restaurants**, and outdoor **markets**.

Shoppers share the streets with **delivery** trucks, workers pushing **handcarts**, and even bicycles.

WILLIAM LOW

Strategy Focus

Every morning, a boy and his grandmother go for a walk in Chinatown. As you read, stop and **summarize** the important parts of the selection.

Reading Restate facts and details (R2.5)

I live in Chinatown with my mother,
father, and grandmother. Our apartment is
above the Chinese American grocery store.

Every morning Grandma and I go for a walk through Chinatown. We hold hands before we cross the street. "Watch out for cars, Grandma," I tell her.

237

Most days the tai chi (tie CHEE) class has already begun by the time we get to the park. Students, young and old, move in the sunlight like graceful dancers.

We always stop and say hello to Mr. Wong, the street cobbler. If our shoes need fixing, Mr. Wong can do the job. "Just like new, and at a good price, too," says Mr. Wong.

Chinatown really wakes up when the delivery trucks arrive. Men with handcarts move quickly over the sidewalks and into the stores.

Every day Grandma and I walk past the Dai-Dai (DYE-dye) Restaurant. Roasted chicken is my favorite, but Grandma likes duck best.

When it gets cold outside and Grandma needs to make medicinal soup, we visit the herbal shop. Inside it is dark and smells musty. The owner, Mr. Chung, is bagging dried roots and herbs.

"Winter is here," says Grandma. "We must get our strength up."

Sometimes Grandma and I go for
lunch at a seafood restaurant. I like to
watch the fish swim in the tank. Grandma
says, "You won't find fresher fish than those
in Chinatown."

The kitchen in the restaurant is a noisy
place. Hot oil sizzles, vegetables crackle,
and woks clang and bang. The cooks
shout to be heard.

At the outdoor market I can barely move. But we go there because Grandma likes to buy fresh snapping crabs for dinner. When the crabs seem furious, Grandma is pleased. "The angrier the crabs, the tastier the meat," she says.

On Saturdays I take lessons at the kung fu school. Master Leung teaches us a new move each week. "To develop your body *and* your mind," says Master Leung, "you must practice every day."

My favorite holiday is Chinese New Year. During the celebrations the streets of Chinatown are always crowded. "Be sure to stay close by," Grandma says.

On New Year's Day the older kids from my kung fu school march to the beat of thumping drums. Grandma and I try to find a good place to watch, and I tell her that next year I'll be marching, too.

255

The New Year's Day parade winds noisily through the streets. "Look, Grandma!" I say. "Here comes the lion."

Firecrackers explode when the lion dance is over. I turn to Grandma, take her hand, and say, "*Gung hay fat choy*, Grandma."

She smiles at me. "And a happy new year to you, too."

Meet the Author and Illustrator
William Low

William Low was born in the Bronx neighborhood of New York City. As a child, he liked to read comics and draw. His neighborhood became one of his favorite things to draw.

Today, Mr. Low works in his studio and teaches art at the New York School of Visual Arts. When he is not painting, he likes to go for walks with his wife, Margaret, and their dog, Sam.

Other books illustrated by William Low:

Good Morning, City
by Elaine Moore
Lily by Abigail Thomas

Internet

If you'd like to learn more about William Low and his artwork, visit Education Place.

www.eduplace.com/kids

Responding

Think About the Selection

1. How does the boy in the story feel about his neighborhood?

2. What does he learn from his grandmother?

3. If you visited Chinatown, what would you most like to see for yourself? Why?

4. What words does the author use to describe how things in Chinatown look, smell, sound, feel, and taste?

5. **Connecting/Comparing** Compare some of the jobs and businesses in *Chinatown* with those in your own community.

Describing

Describe Your Favorite Restaurant

The boy in *Chinatown* likes eating at restaurants. Describe your own favorite restaurant.

Tips

- **Write a title for your description.**
- **Use adjectives to add details to your writing.**

Social Science
Writing

Buyers and sellers (HSS2.4.2)
Write a description (W2.1.b)

Health

Identify Healthful Activities

The characters in *Chinatown* do things to help them stay healthy. Explain how these activities are healthful.

Bonus Keep a log of all the healthful activities you do during one day.

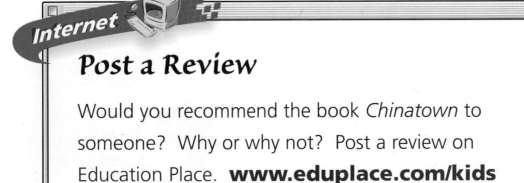

Listening and Speaking

Make Street Sounds

In a small group, think of the different sounds you might hear in Chinatown. Draw pictures of things that make sounds, such as clanging pans. Write words that stand for the sounds. Take turns holding up your pictures and making the sounds.

Internet

Post a Review

Would you recommend the book *Chinatown* to someone? Why or why not? Post a review on Education Place. **www.eduplace.com/kids**

Skill: How to Read a Diagram

❶ Read any captions or labels carefully.

❷ If there are numbered steps to follow, read each step in order.

❸ Reread the instructions for each step before you do it.

California Standards

Standards to Achieve

Reading

• Information from visuals (R2.7)

• Follow written instructions (R2.8)

Math

• Arrange shapes (MMG2.2)

Make a Tangram

by Margaret Kenda and Phyllis S. Williams

With most puzzles, you can put the pieces together in only one right way. With a *tangram*, you can put the pieces together in hundreds of ways.

The tangram idea comes from China. The first book to mention tangrams was published there in 1813, but the idea may be much older. No one really knows. That's part of the mystery of the tangram.

The seven pieces of a real tangram are called *tans*.

To make a tangram, use construction paper, posterboard, or other heavy paper. You may even want to cut out the tangram pieces in different colors.

Here's how to cut a square into the seven tans of a tangram:

 1. Begin with a square.

 2. Cut the square into two large triangles.

 3. Fold one of these triangles in half, and cut it along the dashed line as shown.

 4. Fold the point of the other large triangle as shown and cut along the fold.

5. Fold the larger piece in half, and cut it into two pieces.

 6. Fold one of the small pieces, and cut it along the dashed line as shown.

 7. Fold the other small piece, and cut it as shown.

Now, see if you can put the tans together to form a square.

Play with a Tangram

Were you able to put the square back together again? Here's how to do it.

The seven pieces are numbered, so you can see where they go.

You can create your own tangram designs, or you can put together designs that other people have invented. The only rule is that you have to use all seven tans.

Here are some designs to try.

A bird flying

A person running

A sailboat

Answers for Tangrams

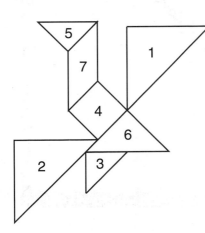

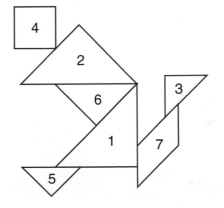

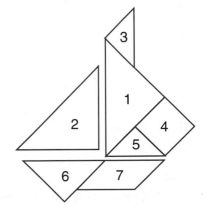

A Friendly Letter

A friendly letter tells a special friend about what you are doing. Use this student's writing as a model when you write a friendly letter of your own.

November 8, 2001

A friendly letter includes a **date**.

Dear Hazel,

A friendly letter has a **greeting**.

I wonder how you are doing. I am doing fine. My apartment is much bigger, including my room. I have a friend already. She is nice. My friend's name is Kate, and she asked me to go to her house. She has a big sister. They gave me something called blondies that were really good.

The main part of the letter is the **body**.

I have another new friend. Her name is Kacy. Kacy and I are buds at afterschool. We work together at homework club.

Writing   **Write a friendly letter (W2.2)**

My teacher is nice. Afterschool art is fun.
It's too bad Kate won't go to afterschool. We
have had a lot of birthdays. I love my new school,
and I like my new apartment too.

Love,
Gaby

Adding **details** makes the letter come alive to the reader.

A friendly letter has a **closing** and the **name** of the writer.

Meet the Author

Gabriela M.
Grade: two
State: Massachusetts
Hobbies: reading, movies, arts and crafts
What she'd like to be when she grows up: a comedian and an artist

California Standards

Standards to Achieve

Reading

- Questions about expository text (R2.4)

Fighting Fires

When a fire happens, every second counts!

At the firehouse, an alarm rings. In the **dispatch** room, an operator tells the **firefighters** exactly where the fire is.

Firefighters quickly put on their special **gear**. They climb onto the **fire engine** and speed away. They're off to take care of an **emergency**!

Learn more about firehouses and fighting fires by reading *A Trip to the Firehouse*.

FIRE DEPARTMENT

Meet the Author

Wendy Cheyette Lewison

Where she was born:
Brooklyn, New York

Other jobs she has had:
Kindergarten teacher;
editor of children's books
and magazines

Her family: She has a husband,
John, and two grown children,
Elizabeth and David.

Other books by Wendy Lewison:
Going to Sleep on the Farm
Hello, Snow!
Buzz Said the Bee

Meet the Photographer

Elizabeth Hathon

Where she lives: On Cape Cod
in Massachusetts, with her
husband and two children

Where she works:
She owns her own photography
business in New York City.

**Other books photographed by
Elizabeth Hathon:**
I Am a Flower Girl
    by Wendy Cheyette Lewison
Daddy and Me
    by Catherine Daly-Weir

Internet

If you want to find out more about the author
and photographer, visit Education Place.
www.eduplace.com/kids

A TRIP to the FIREHOUSE

By Wendy Cheyette Lewison
Photographs by Elizabeth Hathon

Strategy Focus

Some children are visiting their neighborhood firehouse. As you read about their visit, think of **questions** to ask about firehouses and firefighters.

David and his class are visiting their neighborhood
firehouse today. That's why David is wearing a special
shirt. It's fire-engine red!

The fire chief himself greets the children at the door. "Welcome to our firehouse, girls and boys," he says. "We have lots of exciting things to show you."

He lets everyone try on a real fire helmet.

Next they meet the firehouse dog. The children guess his name. They guess right — it's Spot!

The firefighters tell them that Spot has not eaten his breakfast yet. Would they like to come inside and feed him? YES, they would!

While Spot is eating, the children look around.
David sees the firefighters' gear on one wall.
Three firefighters show how long it takes for them to
put it all on. Less than thirty seconds! ▸

Katelyn finds the firehouse pole. "Hello-o-o, down there!" calls a firefighter way up at the top. He grabs the pole with his hands and legs, and slides down — *whoosh!*

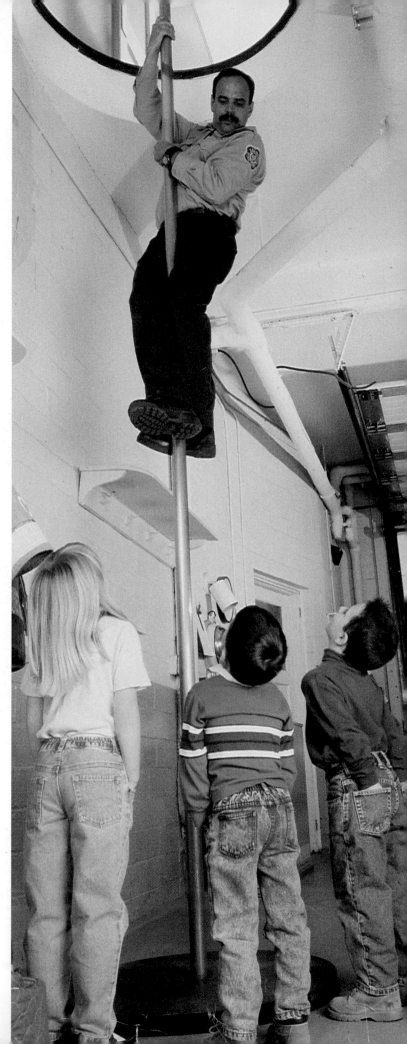

The pole is an important part of the firehouse, he explains. It helps the firefighters move fast when the alarm rings. It is much faster than going down steps. When there's a fire, every second counts!

Josh points to the hole in the ceiling. "What's up there?" he wants to know.

"You can see for yourself," says the firefighter. He leads the children upstairs.

They see where the firefighters sleep. There's a bed, a lamp, and a locker for clothes. There's even a bed for Spot.

There's a kitchen, too, where the firefighters can make themselves something to eat — and maybe share exciting stories when things are slow.

Next the children are taken to see the dispatch room. Things are never slow here!

It is busy all day and all night. Computer monitors flash. Telephone switchboards ring. It is here that phone calls come in, telling operators where the fires are.

Some calls come from 911, the number many communities use for emergencies.

It is here also that alarms come in.

An operator shows the children how the system works. Someone spots a fire and pulls a lever on an alarm box. That makes this bell clang — right here in the firehouse!

The bell clangs a certain number of times, in a pattern or code. The code is punched out on this tape, so it can be seen and recorded.

The operators look up the code on this big blackboard to find out which alarm box the alarm is coming from. Then they know exactly where to send the fire trucks.

Different kinds of fire trucks do different things. Some help at forest fires. Some help at fires in tall buildings. They carry different kinds of special equipment.

Many of these fire trucks are kept at other firehouses. But all are in perfect condition, ready to go, whenever and wherever they are needed.

Aerial Ladder Truck

Ambulance

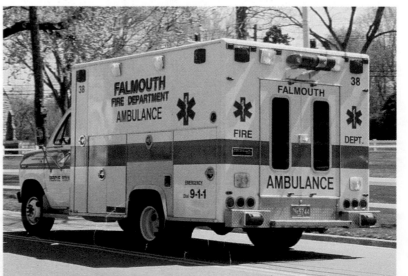

Brush Breaker

Heavy-Duty
Rescue Truck

Dive/Water Rescue Truck

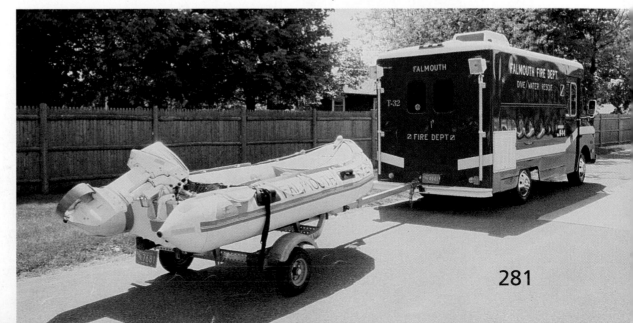

281

The children go downstairs now to get a good look at a fire truck that is kept at this firehouse. They climb all over it, outside and inside.

They pretend they are real firefighters, steering the big engine down the streets of town and calling the dispatch room on the two-way radio.

They examine the bell that clangs, the siren that screams, the hoses that whoosh, the valves that click.

Everything needs to be kept in perfect working order. All the parts need to be checked, and checked again.

The fire truck needs to be clean, too. And since it's such a nice day today, the children are invited to help. They soap it up and rinse it off.

Everyone has fun. Spot has fun, too, playing ball with one of the firefighters!

When the children are done with the washing,
they help a firefighter roll up a long, flat fire hose.
Katelyn thinks it looks just like a snail!

Then the rolled-up hose is stored on the truck
with other hoses — ready to use at a fire.

The firefighters tell the children they've done a great job. They deserve a special treat — bagels and cream cheese in the firehouse kitchen! Yum!

The firefighters and the children are just finishing up their snack, when — *clang! clang!* — the alarm rings!

In a flash, all the firefighters get up and rush out of the room.

Down the pole! Into their gear!

The children watch out the window while the firefighters scramble onto the fire engine.

Off they go down the street. *Whoo-ee! Whoo-ee!*

The children wave. They are sorry their visit to the firehouse is over. But they know the firefighters have a big job to do.

They hope this fire can be put out fast. And most of all, the children hope they are invited back to the firehouse soon!

Responding

Think About the Selection

1. Why do things in the firehouse need to be kept in perfect working order?

2. What do you think is the most difficult part of being a firefighter?

3. Why do you think this selection uses photographs instead of drawings?

4. Would you like to be a firefighter when you grow up? Why or why not?

5. **Connecting/Comparing** How do firefighters help their communities?

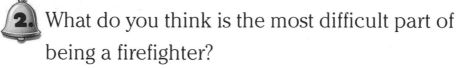

Explaining

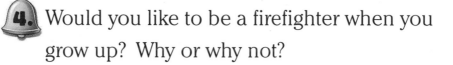

Write Questions and Answers

Think about what you've learned about firefighters and firehouses. Write five questions that visitors to a firehouse might ask. Then write an answer for each question.

Tips

- **Think of questions a firefighter could answer.**
- **End each question with a question mark.**

Reading Author's purpose (R2.3)
Questions about expository text (R2.4)

Estimate Time

It takes less than thirty seconds for a firefighter in the firehouse to get dressed. Think of simple activities that can be done in thirty seconds or less. Act them out with a partner. Use a clock with a second hand to time yourselves.

Make a Glossary

Find words in the story that tell about firehouses. Make a list of at least five words. Then put them in ABC order. Write the meaning of each word next to the word.

Bonus Write sample sentences for your words.

Label a Web Diagram

Print a diagram of a fire truck from Education Place.

Label the parts. You can color it too!

www.eduplace.com/kids

Fire-Safety Tips

by Martin C. Grube

Talk over these fire-safety tips with your whole family. How many do they already know?

Test Your Smoke Detector

Every home should have at least one battery-operated smoke detector on every level of the home and in or near all sleeping areas. Ask a parent to test the smoke detector monthly and to replace the battery with a new one once a year.

Stop, Drop, and Roll

If your clothes catch fire, don't run. Instead, stop where you are; drop to the ground, covering your face with your hands; and roll back and forth on the ground to smother the flames.

Practice Fire Drills

Ask your parents to develop a home fire escape plan with everyone in the household. Have a home fire drill at least twice a year, so the whole family can practice what to do if there is ever a fire. Talk ahead of time about what to do. Agree on where you will all meet outside — away from the home.

Then practice the fire drill: With everyone lying in bed, someone sounds the alarm.

Get up and feel the door to see if it is hot. If it is, use your secondary exit route to escape. If the door is not hot, check the hall for heat or signs of smoke.

If you must go through smoke, crawl low on hands and knees where the air is cleaner. (To avoid dangerous gases and heat that a fire causes near the ceiling, never stand up in smoke.)

See how long it takes for everyone to meet out front at the designated spot.

Costumes and Disguises

In the next story, a class is planning to put on a play. Actors and actresses in a play dress up to look like different characters.

This actor is dressed up to look like a **handsome** prince. The cape is part of his **costume**.

A **mustache** and
bushy wig can be
a good **disguise**.

An actress checks her
make-up in a **mirror**.

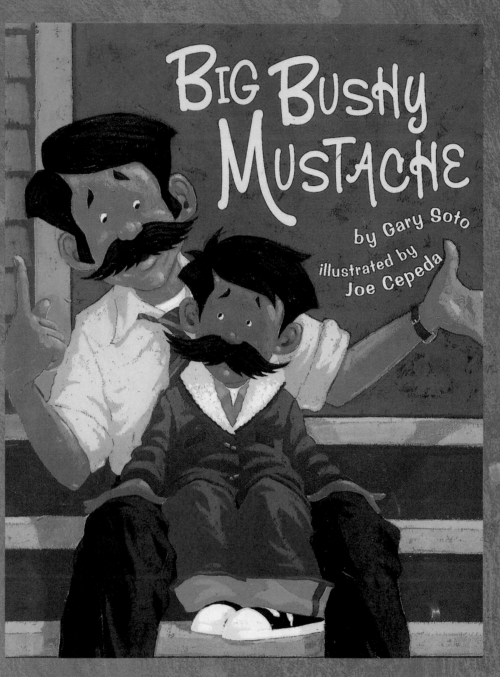

Big Bushy Mustache

by Gary Soto

illustrated by Joe Cepeda

Problems start when Ricky gets a part in a school play. As you read, try to **predict** how the problems will be solved.

Reading   State purpose in reading (R2.2)

People always said Ricky looked just like his mother.

"He has beautiful eyes, exactly like yours, Rosa!" said Mrs. Sanchez, the crossing guard, as his mother took him to school one morning.

"Thanks!" Ricky's mother shouted, and turned a big smile on him. "Have a good day, *mi'jo* (ME-ho)." Then she gave him a kiss.

Ricky went into school frowning. He was a boy. Why didn't people say he looked like his father?

299

That morning his teacher, Mrs. Cortez, brought out
a large box from the closet and set it on her desk. She
took out a hat and a *sarape*. She took out a sword and
raised it toward the ceiling.

"Class, for our next unit we're going to do a play
about *Cinco de Mayo*. That's a holiday that celebrates
the Mexican victory over the French army."

Mrs. Cortez looked around the room. Her eyes settled on Ricky. "Ricky, do you want to carry the sword?"

Ricky shook his head no.

"Do you want to wear this white shirt?"
she asked.

Again Ricky shook his head no. And he shook his
head to the sombrero, the captain's hat, the purple
cape, the tiny Mexican flag.

But when Mrs. Cortez took out a big, bushy mustache, something clicked. This time Ricky nodded yes.

For the rest of the day, the class practiced their
parts. Some of the children played Mexican soldiers.
Some of the children played French soldiers.

All the while, Ricky played with his mustache. It
tickled his lip. It made him feel tough.

When school was over, Mrs. Cortez told the class to leave the costumes in their desks.

Ricky took off his mustache. But instead of leaving it behind, he put it in his pocket. He wanted to take it home. He wanted to surprise his father when he got home from work.

Maybe Mami will take a picture of us, he thought. *We could stand next to each other in front of our new car.*

After Ricky left the school, he pressed the
mustache back onto his lip. He felt grown-up.

A man on the street called out, "Hello, soldier."

Ricky passed a woman carrying groceries. She said,
"What a handsome young man."

He passed a kindergartner, who said, "Mister, would you help me tie my shoes?"

Ricky laughed and ran home. He climbed the wooden steps, pushed open the door, and rushed into the kitchen, where his mother was peeling apples.

"*¡Hola, Mami!*" he said. "I'm hungry."

He looked up and waited for her to say something about his big, bushy mustache.

But she only smiled and handed him a slice of apple.

"*Mi'jo*, wash your hands and help me with the apples," she said.

Ricky's smile disappeared. Didn't she notice?

"Look, Mami. Isn't my *bigote* (be-GO-teh) great?" he said, tugging at her apron.

His mother looked at him.

"¿*Bigote*? What are you talking about?"

"This one," he said. He touched his lip, but the mustache was gone! He felt around his face. It was not on his cheek. It was not on his chin. He looked down to the floor, but it wasn't there, either.

I must have lost it on the way home, Ricky thought.
Without saying anything, he ran out the front door.

He retraced his steps, eyes wide open. He dug
through a pile of raked leaves. He parted the tall grass
that grew along a fence. He looked in the street,
between parked cars, and in flower beds.

He jumped with hope when he saw a black thing.
But when he bent over to pick it up, he discovered that
it was a squashed crayon.

Ricky sat on the curb and cried. The mustache
was gone.

When he got home, Ricky told his mother what had happened. She wiped her hands on a dish towel and hugged him.

At dinner, he wanted to tell Papi too, but the words would not come out. They were stuck in his throat.

He watched his father's big, bushy mustache move up and down when he chewed.

Under his breath, Ricky whispered, "Mustache," but his father didn't hear. He talked about his work.

After dinner, Ricky went to his bedroom. With a
black crayon, he colored a sheet of paper and then cut
it into the shape of a mustache. He taped it to his
mouth and stood before the mirror. But it didn't look
real. He tore it off, crumpled it, and tossed it on
the floor.

In the closet, Ricky found a can of black shoe polish. He looked in the mirror and smeared a line above his lip, but it was too flat, not thick and bushy at all.

Finally, he dug out a pair of old shoes. The strings were black. He cut them in short strips and bound them together with a rubber band. He held the creation above his lip. It looked like a black mop. And smelled like old socks.

That night, after he put on his pajamas, Ricky went into the living room, where his father was listening to the radio. "Papi, I lost my mustache . . .
mi bigote."

His father laughed. "What mustache?"

Ricky climbed into his father's lap and told him
everything. His father smiled and told him a story
about a hen that tried to become a swan. It was a good
story, but it still didn't solve his problem. Tomorrow
he would have to face Mrs. Cortez.

The next morning, Ricky got out of bed slowly. He dressed slowly. He combed his hair slowly. At breakfast, he chewed his cereal slowly. He raised his eyes slowly when his father came into the kitchen.

"*Buenos días,*" he greeted Ricky.

Then Ricky's mother came into the kitchen.

"*Mi'jo,* I have a surprise for you," she said.

323

Mami held out a closed fist and let it open like a flower. Sitting in her palm was a mustache. It was big and bushy.

"You found it!" Ricky shouted happily.

"Well, yes and no," Mami said as she poured herself a cup of coffee.

Ricky pressed the new mustache to his lip.
He ate his cereal, and the mustache moved up and
down, just like his father's.

But something was different about his father's
smile. His lip looked funny. Ricky jumped up and
threw his arms around Papi's neck.

"*Gracias*, Papi! Thank you!" he cried.

"That's okay," Papi told him. "But next time listen to your teacher."

Then Papi touched his son's hair softly. "And, hey, now I look just like you!" Ricky grinned a mile wide.

When Ricky walked to school, he carried the mustache not on his lip, but safely in his pocket.

It wasn't just a bushy disguise anymore, but a gift from his papi.

Meet the Author
Gary Soto

Gary Soto grew up in Fresno, California. When he was nineteen, he thought he might like to be a writer. He has since written many books for children and adults.

Mr. Soto teaches creative writing at the University of California in Berkeley. He has produced films for children, and runs a reading program for community-college students in California.

Meet the Illustrator
Joe Cepeda

Joe Cepeda's son was born while he was working on the illustrations for *Big Bushy Mustache*. He drew his family into the illustration on page 315. That's Mr. Cepeda, his wife, and his son looking over the fence!

Some other books by Gary Soto and Joe Cepeda:
Cat's Meow
The Old Man and His Door

Internet

To read more about this fantastic book-making team, visit Education Place. **www.eduplace.com/kids**

Responding

Think About the Selection

1. How do you think Ricky felt when he realized that he'd lost the mustache?

2. What do you think Ricky learned from this experience?

3. What would you do if you lost something that belonged to your classroom?

4. What if Ricky's father had not given him his mustache? How would the story be different?

5. **Connecting/Comparing** Compare Ricky's neighborhood to the boy's neighborhood in *Chinatown*.

Expressing

Write a Dialogue

Write a dialogue between Ricky and his teacher. Have Ricky explain what happened to the mustache. You may want to role-play your dialogue with a partner.

Tips

- **Look at dialogue in the story.**
- **Use quotation marks before and after spoken words.**

Reading — Impact of alternative endings (R3.2)
Language — Use quotation marks (LC1.5)

Social Studies

Make a Job Toolbox

Make a list of community helpers found in the story. Pick one of the jobs, or think of another type of community helper. Find a small box to use as a toolbox. Then fill it with the things someone would need to do the job you've picked. Draw or cut out pictures of tools.

Viewing

Look at Photographs

Find photographs of men with mustaches. Look in magazines or catalogs. Look for different shapes and colors of mustaches. Then make a Mustaches poster.

Internet

E-Mail a Friend

What did you like about *Big Bushy Mustache*? What didn't you like? Send an e-mail to a friend. Tell your friend about the story.

Family Poems

Sick Days

On days when I am sick in bed
My mother is so nice;
She brings me bowls of chicken soup
And ginger ale with ice.

She cuts the crusts off buttered toast
And serves it on a tray
And sits down while I eat it
And doesn't go away.

She reads my favorite books to me;
She lets me take my pick;
And everything is perfect —
Except that I am sick!

by Mary Ann Hoberman

Thinking Time

Our television's broken,
There's silence in the air,
Silence in the living room,
Silence everywhere.

It gives my brain a time to think,
My eyes a time to see —
I love this silent evening time,
Just family and me.

by Patricia Hubbell

Families,
Families

FAMILIES, FAMILIES
All kinds of families.
Mommies and daddies,
Sisters and brothers,
Aunties and uncles,
     And cousins, too.

People who live with us,
People who care for us,
Grandmas and grandpas,
     And babies, brand new.

FAMILIES, FAMILIES
All kinds of families.
Coming and going,
Laughing and singing,
Caring and sharing,
     And loving you.

*by Dorothy and Michael
Strickland*

334

Subway Travel

Times 42 Str

Not all trains run above the ground. In some big cities, **subway** trains go underground. They travel in tunnels all across the city.

Subway **stations** are places where subway trains stop to pick up people and drop them off. In the story you are about to read, a special event takes place inside a subway station.

A token is a type of coin used to pay for a trip on a subway train.

Tokens are sold in token booths.

Meet the Author
Amy Hest

Before becoming a writer, Amy Hest was a children's librarian. "All my life, though, I secretly wanted to write children's books." Ms. Hest was born in New York City. She still lives there, less than half a block from Sheila White Samton.

Meet the Illustrator
Sheila White Samton

Sheila White Samton can see Amy Hest's building from her apartment window. "We didn't know each other before doing the book, but now we run into each other all the time."

Other books by Sheila White Samton:

Ten Tiny Monsters: A Superbly Scary Story of Subtraction

Frogs in Clogs

Internet

Would you like to learn more about the author and the illustrator of this book? Visit Education Place. **www.eduplace.com/kids**

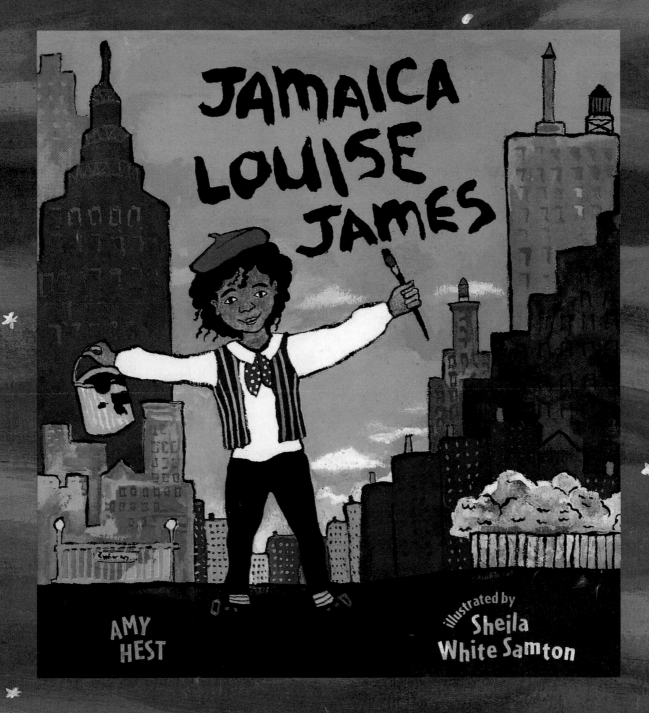

JAMAICA LOUISE JAMES

AMY HEST

illustrated by Sheila White Samton

Jamaica Louise makes her community a happier place. As you read, **evaluate** how well you like the story and the characters.

I was the one with the COOL idea...

It happened last winter and the mayor put my name on a golden plaque. It's down in the subway station at 86th and Main. You can see it if you go there.

JAMAICA
LOUISE
JAMES,
AGE 8

86

That's me. You better believe it!
Want to hear my big idea?

I'll tell but you've got to listen to the whole story, not just a part of it. Mama says my stories go on . . . and on . . . . Whenever I'm just at the beginning of one, she tells me, "Get to the point, Jamaica!" or "Snap to it, baby!" But I like lacing up the details, this way and that.

MAMA

GRAMMY

JAMAICA
LOUISE
JAMES

343

This story begins with me. I have a big artist pad with one hundred big pages and five colored pencils with perfect skinny points.

Sometimes I set myself up on the top step of our building, where everyone can see me. Everything I see is something I want to draw.

HOT DOGS
$1.00

PizzA PaLace

Jamaica, age 7

At night, Mama and Grammy and I cuddle on the couch while the city quiets down. I show them every picture every night.

Sometimes I tell a story as I go. Sometimes they ask a question like, Why does the man's coat have triangle pockets? Other times we don't say a word.

Now look at me on birthday #8. Grammy and Mama dance around my bed. "Open your present!" they shout. "We can't wait another minute!"

Know what they did? They bought me a real paint set — with eight little tubes of color and two paint brushes. Paint sets cost a lot, I worry.

"My! My!" they say. "Are you going to spend birthday #8 WORRYING, when you can be doing something wonderful such as PAINTING THE WORLD?"

So that's when I get my BIG idea.

Now, this part of the story tells about my grammy, who leaves for work when it is still dark. Sometimes I wake up halfway when she slides out of bed. In winter she gets all layered, starting with the long-underwear layer.

She and Mama whisper in the kitchen. They drink that strong black coffee. Grammy scoops up her brown lunch bag and goes outside.

I'm scared in the night. Not Grammy. At 86th and Main she goes down . . . and down . . . into the subway station.

All day long people line up at Grammy's token booth. They give her a dollar or four quarters, and she slides a token into their hand. Then they rush off to catch the train.

Now, I like subways because the seats are hot pink and because they go very fast. But I don't like subway stations. Especially the one at 86th and Main. There are too many steep steps (fifty-six) and too many grownups who all look mad. The walls are old tile walls without any color.

When Grammy comes home, she sews and talks about the people she sees, like Green-Hat Lady or Gentleman with the Red Bow Tie. Mama reads and hums.

But I paint, blending all those colors until they look just right. Every day I add a picture to my collection and every day I think about my cool idea.

At last it's the morning of Grammy's birthday.
Mama and I get up early. We get all layered and
sneak outside. Mama holds my hand. I am scared
but also VERY EXCITED.

We swoosh along in our boots in the dark
in the snow. At 86th and Main we go down . . .

and down . . .

fifty-six steep steps.

3111

We don't buy a token at the token booth. We
don't take a ride on the subway. What we do is hang
a painting on the old tile wall. Then another. And
another . . . and one more. Before you know it, that
station is all filled up with color.

Surprise!

we shout when Grammy comes clomping down the steps.

She looks all around that station. "Jamaica Louise James," she calls, "come right here so I can give you a big hug, baby!"

JAMAICA
LOUISE
JAMES,
AGE 8

362

So now you know the whole story. Everyone
sure is in love with my subway station! You'd be
surprised. People are talking to each other — some
even smile. "That looks like me!" says a lady in a
green hat to a gentleman with a red bow tie.

Then Grammy tells everyone about Jamaica
Louise James, age 8.

THAT'S ME. YOU BETTER BELIEVE IT!

Responding

Think About the Selection

1. When does Jamaica Louise first think of her big idea?

2. How does Grammy feel about Jamaica Louise's big idea? How do you know?

3. Why do you think the grownups on the subway look mad?

4. Would you like to be friends with Jamaica Louise? Why or why not?

5. **Connecting/Comparing** In what ways is Jamaica Louise's grandmother like the grandmother in *Chinatown*? How are they different?

Narrating

Write a Story

Grammy tells Jamaica Louise about people at the subway station. Choose a person from the station, such as the Green-Hat Lady. Write a story about that person.

Tips

- **Think up a name for your character.**
- **List words that describe him or her.**

Reading — Compare story elements (R3.1)
Writing — Organize related ideas (W1.1)

Draw Pictures for Your Community

Jamaica Louise draws pictures that make people smile. Draw pictures that will make people in your community smile. Think of places where you might want to put your art.

Speak to Give a Reason

Jamaica Louise's cool idea was a success. Think of a cool idea to help your community. Think of what you would say to the mayor to convince him or her that your idea will work. Practice your speech with a partner.

Internet

Make an Online Plaque

The mayor liked Jamaica Louise's big idea so much that he had her name put on a plaque. Print a plaque from Education Place. Fill it in for yourself or for someone else.

www.eduplace.com/kids

Listening/Speaking

Present organized ideas (LS1.5)
Speak clearly/appropriately (LS1.6)

Skill: How to Follow a Recipe

Before you begin . . .

❶ Find an adult to work with you.

❷ Read the recipe carefully.

❸ Gather the ingredients and the tools you'll need.

While you work . . .

❶ Reread each step.

❷ Follow the steps in the correct order.

California Standards

Standards to Achieve

Reading

• **Follow written instructions (R2.8)**

Sidewalk Sticks

by Marie E. Cecchini

Here's a recipe for homemade sidewalk chalk that's as much fun to make as it is to use.

What you'll need:

8 white eggshells

4 teaspoons hot water

red, yellow, and blue food coloring

4 teaspoons flour

mortar and pestle or aluminum pie tin and medium-sized stone

small bowl

wire whisk

spatula

foil

What to do:

1. Carefully clean and dry eggshells. Place a few shells at a time in mortar and use pestle to grind into powder. Or put eggshells in pie tin and grind them with stone. It may take a few minutes to grind eggshells completely.

2. Put 1 teaspoon hot water into small bowl. Add 1 or 2 drops food coloring.

3. Add 1 teaspoon flour to water and food coloring and stir well with whisk.

4. Add 1 tablespoon eggshell powder and stir with whisk until mixture is well blended and sticky.

5. Use a spatula to scrape mixture out of bowl and into your hands. Firmly shape the mixture into a stick. Set finished stick on a piece of foil to dry. Thoroughly rinse and dry bowl.

   Repeat steps 2 through 5 until you have 4 chalk sticks. Your chalk will take 2 or 3 days to dry once you've shaped it.

✔ # Writing a Personal Response

Some tests ask you to choose an idea and write what you think about it. Here is a sample.

Tips

- Read the directions carefully.
- Look for key words that tell you what to write about.
- Decide which idea you will write about.
- Plan your answer before you start to write.

Choose one idea to write about. Write at least one paragraph.

a. Many of the characters in the theme *Around Town: Neighborhood and Community* visit special places in their communities. What are some of your favorite places to go in your community? Why?

b. What do you like about your neighborhood? Why?

Writing   **Organize related ideas (W1.1)**

Now look at a good answer that one student wrote.

There are many places I like to go in my community. My favorite place to go is the Play and Learn Space. I like to go to there because they have a huge game room, a library, and even a TV and video room.

My second favorite place to go is the youth center. I like it because Ms. Fisher is there. She is nice to everyone and always has a lot of good ideas for activities. I really enjoy Tuesdays there because they are Project Days.

The answer stays on the topic.

The answer has describing and exact words.

The answer is well organized.

There are few mistakes in grammar, spelling, capitalization, or punctuation.

Glossary

This glossary can help you find the meanings of some of the words in this book. The meanings given are the meanings of the words as they are used in the book. Sometimes a second meaning is also given.

A

apartment

One or more rooms in a house or building used as a place to live: *There are six rooms in our apartment.*

B

backpack

A bag worn on the back to carry things: *My backpack is very heavy because it has so many things in it.*

backpack

balance

To have the correct amounts of: *We could not balance the teeter-totter because one end was too heavy.*

balanced

A form of **balance**: *A balanced meal includes many different kinds of food.*

bank

The sloping ground along the edge of a river or lake: *Many trees and bushes grow along this bank of the river.*

booth

A small stand where things are shown or sold: *Six people stood in line at the ticket booth.*

bushy

Thick and shaggy: *The dog's hair was so bushy you couldn't see its eyes!*

C

camp

To stay outdoors in shelters such as tents or cabins: *My parents bought a tent because we love to **camp**.*

campfire

An outdoor fire used for warmth or cooking: *Angela's mother built a **campfire** to cook dinner.*

campfire

camping

A form of **camp**: *We packed food and other supplies for our **camping** trip.*

celebration

A party or other activity to honor a special day: *Birthday parties are my favorite kind of **celebration**.*

chief

A person who leads other people: *The **chief** was in charge of all the officers at the police station.*

commotion

Noisy activity; confusion: *The **commotion** made by people talking and laughing woke the baby.*

costume

Special clothing worn by someone in a play or dressing up like someone else: *Ana and her friends wore flower **costumes** to the party.*

crater

A hollow area in the ground, shaped like a bowl: *The elephant's foot made a **crater** in the ground.*

crumb

A tiny piece of food, often of bread or cake: *People threw bread **crumbs** to the ducks in the pond.*

D

dairy

Foods that are made with milk, cream, butter, or cheese: *Milk, cheese, and other **dairy** foods come from cows and goats.*

dairy foods

deliver

To take something from one place to another: *Will you **deliver** this pizza to the next classroom, please?*

delivered

Form of **deliver**: *The mail carrier **delivered** our mail at noon today.*

delivery

Having to do with an object or person that delivers: *A **delivery** truck brought our new stove to the house.*

diet

The food and drink that a person or animal usually has: *A healthful **diet** includes lots of fruits and vegetables.*

disguise

Clothes and make-up worn to make a person look like someone else: *The clown at Tony's party was really his father in **disguise**.*

dispatch

1. To send something quickly to a certain place or person: *The operator can **dispatch** a message to the firefighters in seconds.*

2. A place where messages come in and go out: *Stan answered phones in the **dispatch** room.*

E

edge

The line or point where an object or area ends: *Jodie sat at the **edge** of the pool and put her feet in the water.*

emergency

A problem that happens suddenly and has to be solved at once: *Firefighters and the police help when **emergencies** happen.*

explore

To go into or travel through a place you have never been before: *I like to **explore** different shelves in the library.*

exploring

Form of **explore**: *During our vacation, my family went **exploring** in old caves.*

F

feather

The light outer covering of a bird: *The bird shook the rain off its **feathers**.*

feather

fire engine

A truck that carries firefighters with their hoses and ladders to fight a fire: *The **fire engine** raced down the road to the fire.*

firefighter

A person who puts out fires for a living: *The **firefighters** used water from their hoses to spray the fire.*

G

gear

Equipment such as tools or clothing used most often for a certain activity: *Football players wear helmets and other **gear** to protect themselves.*

football gear

H

habitat

The place where an animal or plant normally lives and grows: *The **habitat** of a panda is a bamboo forest.*

handcart

A small cart pushed or pulled by the hand: *The workers moved all of the boxes with **handcarts**.*

handsome

Pleasing to look at: *Billy looked very **handsome** with his new haircut.*

hike

1. To go on a long walk: *My family likes to **hike** on the paths around South Lake.*
2. A long walk: *Walking around the whole lake was quite a **hike** for one day.*

hungry

Wanting to eat: *Running and playing made the children **hungry**.*

I

imitation

The act of copying the looks, sounds, or actions of something or someone: *Lucy can do a good **imitation** of our dog barking.*

L

lantern

A hand-held container for holding a light, with sides that let the light shine through: *When we go camping, we use our **lantern** to read at night.*

lantern

M

market

A public place where people buy and sell goods: *Tom's father buys apples at the **market** to make pies.*

mirror

A piece of glass that you can see yourself in: *Maria looked in the **mirror** to see her new hat.*

mirror

moss

Small green or brown plants that grow close together like carpet on the ground, rocks, and trees: *Some **moss** is growing in the shady area under that tree.*

moss

mustache

The hair growing on a person's upper lip: *Whenever our teacher drinks milk, he gets some on his **mustache**.*

N

noise

One or more loud sounds: *The car horns made so much **noise** they woke me up.*

P

path

A place where you can walk through a field or forest: *The cleared **path** in the woods made walking easy.*

plaque

A flat piece of wood, metal, or stone that has words on it about a person or event: *Russell was given a **plaque** with his name on it for winning the contest.*

protect

To keep safe: *Sunglasses **protect** your eyes from bright sunlight.*

R

ranger

A person who works in and watches over a forest or park: *The park **ranger** gave my mother good directions.*

ranger

release

To set free: *I'm going to **release** the caterpillar I caught.*

released

Form of **release**: *The boy released the bird from the cage.*

restaurant

A place where people go to eat meals: *Instead of cooking, Mr. Chen ate dinner at a restaurant.*

S

shallow

Not deep: *We can walk along the edge of the lake, where the water is shallow.*

shop

To go to stores to look at or buy things: *We go once a week to shop for food at the grocery store.*

shopper

A person who goes to stores to look at or buy things: *Only one shopper was in the store all afternoon.*

shopping

Form of **shop**: *Jack went shopping for a new shirt.*

sign

A thing that something does that can help you learn about it: *The dog's movements were signs that it wanted to play.*

slurp

To drink or sip something noisily: *My mother doesn't like it when I slurp my soup.*

slurped

Form of **slurp**: *Nadia slurped her chocolate milkshake until it was all gone.*

spread

To open out wide or wider: *The painter spread old newspaper on the floor in case the paint spilled.*

station

1. A stopping place along a route for taking on and letting off passengers: *We got off at the wrong* **station** *and had to wait for another train.*

2. A place or building where community helpers work: *The fire trucks drove into the fire* **station**.

station

subway

A train that travels through underground tunnels: *Mrs. Sanders takes the* **subway** *to and from work everyday.*

T

tent

A place to sleep when you camp, usually made of cloth and held up with poles: *Sheila taught Robbie how to set up his* **tent** *at the camp.*

tent

tire

To make or become weak from work or effort: *Our legs began to* **tire** *from the long walk home.*

token

A piece of stamped metal that is used instead of money, as on buses and subways: *We had to buy a **token** to get on the bus.*

token

tour

A brief trip through a place in order to see and learn about it: *The students enjoy going on **tours** of the new space museum.*

U

urban

Part of, about, or placed in the city: *Travis moved away from the country to live in an **urban** area.*

V

vegetable

A plant or plant part that is used as food: *I like orange **vegetables** such as carrots and sweet potatoes.*

vegetables

W

wear

To have on the body: *I think I will **wear** my new coat outside today.*

wearing

Form of **wear**: *Melissa was **wearing** a pretty red dress at the party.*

Acknowledgments

Main Literature Selections

Around the Pond: Who's Been Here?, by Lindsay Barrett George. Copyright © 1996 by Lindsay Barrett George. Reprinted by permission of HarperCollins Publishers.

Big Bushy Mustache, by Gary Soto, illustrated by Joe Cepeda. Text copyright © 1998 by Gary Soto. Illustrations copyright © 1998 by Joe Cepeda. Reprinted by permission of Alfred A. Knopf, a division of Random House Inc.

Chinatown, text and illustrations, by William Low. Copyright © 1997 by William Low. Reprinted by permission of Henry Holt and Company, LLC.

"Shopping," from *Dragon Gets By,* by Dav Pilkey. Copyright © 1991 by Dav Pilkey. Reprinted by permission of Orchard Books, New York.

Exploring Parks with Ranger Dockett, by Alice K. Flanagan, photographs by Christine Osinski. Copyright © 1997 by Alice K. Flanagan and Christine Osinski. Reprinted by permission of Children's Press, a division of Grolier Publishing.

Henry and Mudge and the Starry Night, by Cynthia Rylant, illustrated by Suçie Stevenson. Text copyright © 1998 by Cynthia Rylant. Illustrations copyright © 1998 by Suçie Stevenson. Reprinted by permission of Simon & Schuster Books for Young Readers, an imprint of Simon & Schuster Children's Publishing Division. All rights reserved.

Jamaica Louise James, by Amy Hest, illustrated by Sheila White Samton. Text copyright © 1996 by Amy Hest. Illustrations copyright © 1996 by Sheila White Samton. Reprinted by permission of Candlewick Press, Inc., Cambridge, MA.

Julius, by Angela Johnson, illustrated by Dav Pilkey. Text copyright ©1993 by Angela Johnson. Illustrations copyright © 1993 by Dav Pilkey. Reprinted by permission of Orchard Books, New York.

Mrs. Brown Went to Town, by Wong Herbert Yee. Copyright © 1996 by Wong Herbert Yee. Reprinted by permission of Houghton Mifflin Company. All rights reserved.

A Trip to the Firehouse, by Wendy Cheyette Lewison, photographs by Elizabeth Hathon. Text copyright © 1998 by Grosset & Dunlap Inc. Photographs copyright © 1998 by Elizabeth Hathon. Reprinted by permission of the Putnam & Grosset Group, a division of Penguin Putnam Inc.

Focus Selections

Selection from *More Fables of Aesop,* by Jack Kent. Text copyright © 1974 by Jack Kent. Reprinted by permission of June Kent.

Links and Theme Openers

"A Neighborhood is a Friendly Place" from the song with words by Ella Jenkins. Copyright © by Ell-Bern Publishing. Reprinted by permission of Ell-Bern Publishing, Chicago, IL. All rights reserved.

"Campfire Games" from *The Kids Campfire Book,* written by Jane Drake and Ann Love and illustrated by Heather Collins. Text and cover reprinted by permission of Kids Can Press Ltd., Toronto, Canada. Text copyright © 1996 by Jane Drake and Ann Love.

"Families, Families" from *Families: Poems Celebrating the African American Experience,* by Dorothy S. Strickland and Michael R. Strickland, published by Boyd's Mills Press, Inc. Text copyright © 1994 by Dorothy S. Strickland and Michael R. Strickland. Reprinted by permission of the publisher.

"Fire-Safety Tips," by Martin C. Grube, reprinted with permission from the October 1998 issue of *Highlights for Children.* Copyright © 1998 by Highlights for Children, Inc., Columbus, Ohio.

"How To Be A Wildlife Spy," by Carolyn Duckworth, from the April 1995 issue of *Ranger Rick* magazine. Copyright © by Carolyn Duckworth. Reprinted by permission of the author.

"It's Easy To Be Polite" from *Soup Should Be Seen, Not Heard!,* by Beth Brainard and Sheila Behr. Copyright © 1990 by The Good Idea Kids, Inc. Reprinted by permission of Dell Publishing, a division of Random House, Inc.

"Looking Around" from *Out in the Dark and Daylight,* by Aileen Fisher. Copyright © 1980 by Aileen Fisher. Reprinted by permission of Marian Reiner for the author.

"Make a Tangram" from *Math Wizardry for Kids.*

Copyright © 1995 by Margaret Kenda and Phyllis Williams. Reprinted by permission of Barron's Educational Series, Inc.

"Oak's Introduction" from *Old Elm Speaks: Tree Poems*, by Kristine O'Connell George, illustrated by Kate Kiesler. Text copyright © 1998 by Kristine O'Connell George. Reprinted by permission of Houghton Mifflin Company.

"Roly-Poly" from *Play and Find Out About Science*, by Janice VanCleave. Text copyright © 1996 by Janice VanCleave. Reprinted by permission of John Wiley & Sons, Inc.

"Sick Days" from *Fathers, Mothers, Sisters, Brothers: A Collection of Family Poems,* by Mary Ann Hoberman. Text copyright © 1991 by Mary Ann Hoberman. Illustrations copyright © 1991 by Marylin Haffner. Reprinted by permission of Little, Brown and Company. (Inc.)

"Sidewalk Sticks," by Marie E. Cecchini. Reprinted by permission of *Spider*, *the Magazine for Children*, July 1998, Vol. 5, No. 7. Copyright © 1998 by Carus Publishing Company.

"Smile" from *Bing Bang Boing*, by Douglas Florian. Copyright © 1994 by Douglas Florian. Reprinted with permission of Harcourt Inc.

"Thinking Time," by Patricia Hubbell. Copyright © 1997 by Patricia Hubbell. Used by permission of Marian Reiner for the author.

Special thanks to the following teachers whose students' compositions appear as Student Writing Models: Cheryl Claxton, Florida; Patricia Kopay, Delaware; Susana Llanes, Michigan; Joan Rubens, Delaware; Nancy Schulten, Kentucky; Linda Wallis, California

Credits

Photography
CA4 (frog) JH Pete Carmichael/ImageBank. **CA5** (piglet) © 2001 PhotoDisc. (butterfly) PhotoSpin. (flag) © Joseph Sohm;ChromoSohm, Inc./CORBIS. **5** images Copyright © 2000 PhotoDisc, Inc.**10** (bkgd) DigitalVision. **10–11** Arthur Tilley/FPG International. **16** (t) Artville. **35** Courtesy Grolier Inc./Orchard Books. **37** (l)

Eyewire. **44–5** Larry Lefever/Grant Heilman Photography **45** (tl) Larry Lefever/Grant Heilman Photography. (tr) Peter Cade/Tony Stone Images. **46** (t) Courtesy Grolier Inc./Orchard Books. (b) Courtesy Grolier Inc./Orchard Books. **75** (b) image Copyright © 2000 PhotoDisc, Inc. **80** (l) Image Farm/PictureQuest. (b) Peter Cade/Tony Stone Images. **81** (tl) Corbis Royalty Free. (tr) Tony Page/Tony Stone Images. (b) Randy Wells/Tony Stone Images. **80–1** (frame) Image Farm. **82** Courtesy Wong Herbert Yee. **83** (bkgd) Image Farm/PictureQuest. **109** (l) image Copyright © 2000 PhotoDisc, Inc. **110** (t) Ron Kimball Photography. (m) Comstock KLIPS (b) Lynn M. Stone. **111** (tl) (tm) (bl) (bm) image Copyright © 2000 PhotoDisc, Inc. (tr) (br) Classic PIO Partners. **114** (icon) image Copyright © 2000 PhotoDisc, Inc. **114–5** Jose L. Pelaez/The Stock Market. **121** (tl) Artville. (tr) Corbis Royalty Free. (b) Rob Walker/Workbook CO/OP Stock. **122** (t) (b) Courtesy Simon & Schuster. **149** (b) Corbis/Peter Johnson. **156** (l) image Copyright © 2000 PhotoDisc, Inc. (br) Corbis/Phil Schermeister. **157** (tl) Corbis/Wolfgang Kaehler. (tr) Keith Wood/Tony Stone Images. (bl) David Young-Wolff/Tony Stone Images. (br) Corbis/Jim Sugar. **158** (t) (b) Christine Osinski. (icon) image Copyright ©2000 PhotoDisc, Inc. **159** (bkgd) image Copyright © 2000 PhotoDisc, Inc. **174** images Copyright © 2000 PhotoDisc, Inc. **175** images Copyright © 2000 PhotoDisc, Inc. **178** (t) image Copyright © 2000 PhotoDisc, Inc. (ml) Stuart Westmorland/Tony Stone Images (mr) Rob Simpson/VALAN Photos. (l) PhotoTone. **179** (bkgd) Willard Clay/FPG International. (bl) Frank Oberle/Tony Stone Images. (bm) John Mitchell/VALAN Photos. (br) Terry Husebye/Tony Stone Images. **180** Mickey Kauffman. (frame) Image Farm. **181** (bkgd) PhotoTone. **204** image Copyright © 2000 PhotoDisc, Inc. **205** (tr) image Copyright © 2000 PhotoDisc, Inc. **206** image Copyright © 2000 PhotoDisc, Inc. **207** (bkgd) Myrleen Cate/IndexStock. (tl) Corbis Royalty Free. (tm) Corbis/Lynda Richardson. (tr) image Copyright © 2000 PhotoDisc, Inc. **208** (t) Roy Morsch/The

Stock Market. (b) CC Lockwood/Animals Animals. **208–9** Lori Adamski Peek/Tony Stone Images. **226** (bkgd) Corbis Royalty Free. (icon) image Copyright © 2000 PhotoDisc, Inc. **226–7** © Joan Steiner. **232** Corbis/Nik Wheeler. **233** (t) Jan Halaska/IndexStock. (b) Corbis/Dave G. Houser. **257** (r) Courtesy of Henry Holt & Company. **268** (l) Courtesy Wendy Lewison. (r) Elizabeth Hathon.**268–9** (bkgd) Bruce Byers 1992/FPG International. **269–89** Elizabeth Hathon.**290** (inset) Elizabeth Hathon. (l) George Shelley/The Stock Market. **290–1** Bruce Byers 1992/FPG International. **329** (l) Carolyn Soto. (r) Michael Justice/Mercury Pictures. **337** (tl) Bud Freund/IndexStock. (tr) Comstock. (b) Jan Halaska/IndexStock. **338** (l) Michael Tamborrino/Mercury Pictures. (r) Courtesy Sheila White Samton. **370** image Copyright © 2000 PhotoDisc, Inc. **371** image Copyright © 2000 PhotoDisc, Inc. **372** Eyewire. **373** Artville. **374** (l) Corbis Royalty Free. **375** image Copyright © 2000 PhotoDisc, Inc. **376** (l) image Copyright © 2000 PhotoDisc, Inc. (r) Photo Sphere Images/PictureQuest. **377** Corbis/Joseph Sohm; ChromoSohm Inc. **379** (l) Corbis/Jan Butchofsky-Houser. (r) Corbis Royalty Free.

Assignment Photography
CA1 (t) Joel Benjamin. (b) Tony Scarpetta. **CA2** (t) Joel Benjamin. (b) Tony Scarpetta. **CA3** Tony Scarpetta. **CA4** (t) Joel Benjamin. (b) Tony Scarpetta. **CA5** Joel Benjamin. **3** Joel Benjamin. **16** (b), **17, 37** (r), **38, 40** (t, mb, b), **41, 76–9, 260–1, 293–4, 296–7, 366–7** Joel Benjamin. **234, 259** (lr), **291** (ml, mr), **330–1, 365** Ken Karp. **120, 150–3** Allan Landau. **113, 211, 369** Tony Scarpetta.

Illustration
10, 223 Bernard Adnet. **76–79** Amanda Haley. **176–177** Jui Ishida. **212–213** Tom Saecher. **215** Craig Spearing. **217** Linda S. Wingerter. **219** Eric Brace. **221** Kumio Hagio. **226–227** Copyright © 2001 Joan Steiner. **266–267** Brian Lies. **268** Jeff Zimmerman. **295** Lauren Scheuer. **329** Melissa Iwai. **332–333** Copyright © 2001 by Margaret Chodes-Irving. **334–335** Copyright © 2001 by Leonard Jenkins. **338, 364** Roxanna Baer.